Moodle Theme Development

Build customized themes to make your Moodle courses engaging and interactive

Silvina Paola Hillar

BIRMINGHAM - MUMBAI

Moodle Theme Development

First published: December 2016

Production reference: 1021216

Published by Packt Publishing Ltd.
Livery Place
35 Livery Street
Birmingham
B3 2PB, UK.

ISBN 978-1-78646-321-0

www.packtpub.com

Credits

Author

Silvina Paola Hillar

Reviewer

Susan Smith Nash

Commissioning Editor

Amarabha Banerjee

Acquisition Editor

Larissa Pinto

Content Development Editor

Onkar Wani

Technical Editor

Rashil Shah

Copy Editor

Safis Editing

Project Coordinator

Ulhas Kambali

Proofreader

Safis Editing

Indexer

Rekha Nair

Graphics

Abhinash Sahu

Production Coordinator

Aparna Bhagat

About the Author

Silvina P. Hillar is Italian and has been teaching English since 1993. She has always had a great interest in teaching and has done a lot of research on teaching methodologies, management techniques and embed them into e-learning and teaching. She has also explored different types of e-learning combining them with Moodle. She also researches on multimedia assets that enhance teaching and learning through VLE platforms. She tries to embed the learning of students through new resources that are appealing and innovative for them. In this way, she ensures that multimedia stimulates different thinking skills as well as multiple types of intelligence.

She is an English teacher, a Certified Legal Translator (English/Spanish), and has a postgraduate degree in Education (graduated with honors).

She has worked at several schools and institutions with native English speaking students and students of English as a foreign language, and as an independent consultant for many international companies in the capacity of an Interpreter, Translator, and **Virtual Learning Environment** (**VLE**) Course Designer.

She has always had a passion for technological devices concerning education. Formerly, videos and cassettes were a must in her teaching lessons; the computer was, and still does, play a big role. Her brother, Gastón C. Hillar, designed some programs and games for her teaching. Lately, she has been teaching using Moodle and the Web. She believes that one of the most amazing challenges in education is bridging the gap between classic education and modern technologies.

She has authored: *Moodle 1.9: The English Teacher's Cookbook, Moodle 2.0 Multimedia Cookbook, Moodle 2.5 Multimedia Cookbook second edition, Mind Mapping with FreeMind and Moodle 2.3 Multimedia Video Course*.

When not tinkering with computers, she enjoys travelling with her son, Nico and her love, Jorge, with whom she spends wonderful time.

Acknowledgements

I'd like to thank all the team members at Packt Publishing, who worked with me as an incredibly helpful team; Larissa Pinto, who trusted me to work on this project--we worked together so that the idea came into this book--and Onkar Wani, who was very patient and helpful with time management. I would like to thank my technical reviewer, Rashil Shah; my reviewer Susan Nash; and proofreaders, for their thorough reviews and insightful comments.

The writing process of a book involves a great amount of lonely hours, therefore, I owe tremendous thanks to my wonderful son, Nico, who was very patient and supportive in the writing process of the book. He was on some occasions forced to be alone while I concentrated on my writing. Special thanks to my love Jorge, who was very supportive during the whole writing process.

My parents, Susana and Jose, who always stand by me and support my decisions. My brother, Gastón C. Hillar ,and his wife, Vanesa Olsen, and my nephews, Brandon and Kevin, with whom I spend unforgettable moments.

Last but not least, I would like to thank the Rivera and Dimuro families, with whom I share delicious asados.

I would also like to thank all my students, either virtual or real, who make it possible for me to be a teacher.

About the Reviewer

Susan Smith Nash has been designing and developing online courses and programs for more than 15 years for education, training, and personal development.

In addition to *Moodle 3.x Teaching Techniques*, Nash is the author of a number of Moodle books and training videos, including *Moodle 3.x Course Design*, *Moodle Course Design Best Practices* and *Moodle for Training and Professional Development*. She has also authored *Video-Assisted Mobile Learning for Writing Courses (2016)*.

Thank you to my online students and also to Dr. Jeff Kissinger, Director of the Rollins College Instructional Design Certificate Program, and Don Tharp, Ashland University.

www.PacktPub.com

For support files and downloads related to your book, please visit www.PacktPub.com.

Did you know that Packt offers eBook versions of every book published, with PDF and ePub files available? You can upgrade to the eBook version at www.PacktPub.com and as a print book customer, you are entitled to a discount on the eBook copy. Get in touch with us at service@packtpub.com for more details.

At www.PacktPub.com, you can also read a collection of free technical articles, sign up for a range of free newsletters and receive exclusive discounts and offers on Packt books and eBooks.

https://www.packtpub.com/mapt

Get the most in-demand software skills with Mapt. Mapt gives you full access to all Packt books and video courses, as well as industry-leading tools to help you plan your personal development and advance your career.

Why subscribe?

- Fully searchable across every book published by Packt
- Copy and paste, print, and bookmark content
- On demand and accessible via a web browser

Dedicated to my beloved son Nico, my nephews Kevin and Brandon, my love Jorge, and his son Agus

Table of Contents

Preface

A long time ago, we could specify the most appropriate resolution where your user can have a nice experience with the website when we designed themes for it. We could design our themes, considering that they will look great for a specific resolution and just include a notice indicating that unless the user displays the website with a resolution of 800-by-600 pixels, it was their fault if they have a horrible user experience. However, those times are over. Nowadays, we have to design themes that are capable of working with different resolutions, screen sizes, screen orientations, and pixel densities. Our themes must be responsive, and the users must be able to have a great user experience, no matter what device they use to access our website.

These requirements are extremely important when we design modern Moodle themes. We cannot use the same recipes that worked OK a few years ago. We need new recipes that consider the requirements for excellent user experiences with any devices. Smartphones, tablets, phablets, ultrabooks, all-in-one computers, retina displays, high-DPI displays, and smartTVs can access our Moodle courses. Our Moodle themes must be ready to provide an excellent user experience in all these displays. We cannot design themes for just a few screen resolutions anymore.

This book will teach you how to design themes, considering all the requirements for what is known as the post-PC era.

When theming, we must bear in mind many items, because we may want to change completely the look and feel of our Moodle course, but first of all we need to organize how to do it. We need to start from some basic concepts to bear in mind before taking the first step. We need to focus on small targets and then on the general look of the course. Therefore, in this book we will cover several aspects that we need to know about theming. We will deal with the free version of MoodleCloud, which has another version that is paid and offers more possibilities than the free one. But throughout the book, when referring it to MoodleCloud, we will be making reference to the free and open source one. Bearing in mind that MoodleCloud is not the only cloud-hosted Moodle hosting, we need to know that there are many services that host Moodle, and so users can download Moodle 3 and install to their own server space and also select a Moodle hosting service--many of which allow one to select from dozens of themes--and the themes are customizable. Whereas in this book, when talking about Moodle we will deal with Moodle on-premises, and we will learn how to customize it.

Through the chapters of the book we will start a journey through the land of theming and we will learn some information that will help us to create, design, and improve the theming of our courses. We will deal with icons, images, screen resolutions, responsive themes, among other relevant items that enhance the Moodle themes. Furthermore, we cover different devices and emulate them in order to check what the theme looks like in them. We learn how to code basic HTML and CSS with the help of online editors that help and teach us how to do it. We learn where to find themes and layouts for the Moodle courses and we also explore how to customize at the MoodleCloud maximum level, taking into account that we deal only with the free and open source version. Last but not least, we put all the pieces together, and in the last chapter we recap everything that we have explored, and we can spice our Moodle Course, with some tips that let us theme our course, adding some blocks, for instance, in order to continue changing the look and feel of our course.

What this book covers

Chapter 1, *An Introduction to Moodle 3 and MoodleCloud*, covers most of what needs to be known about e-learning, VLEs, Moodle, and MoodleCloud. There is a slight difference in between Moodle and MoodleCloud, especially if you don't have access to a Moodle course in the institution where you are working and want to design a Moodle course. Furthermore, Moodle is used on different devices, and there are several aspects to take into account when designing a course and building a Moodle theme for these devices. We have also dealt with screen resolution, aspect ratio, types of images, and texts and anti-aliasing effects.

Chapter 2, *Themes in Moodle 3 on-premises and MoodleCloud*, shows what themes are and how to find them in Moodle and in MoodleCloud. We also reveal a little about HTML code and how colors are named in this code. We customize the Moodle theme called More and find out where our Moodle themes are on our computer. We have search for, download, and install Moodle theme Essential. We deal with plenty of information relevant to Moodle themes and where to find it.

Chapter 3, *Setting Up Logos in Moodle Themes*, works with UI-based settings to tune our Moodle themes. We do not change specific files such as HTML files or CSS because we take advantage of a theme where we can design a logo using on online logo editor, upload a logo, Favicon, background image as a tiled style. Regarding MoodleCloud, we learn how to upload a logo that can be seen in the header of the front page and the header of the login page, which is allowed in the theme that we are working with, bearing in mind that MoodleCloud has some limitations.

`Chapter 4`, *Customizing the Header and the Footer*, explain how to add images and text to the footer and the header. Hence, we add hyperlinks to social networks in Moodle on-premises. Apart from that, we can add a slide show and modify the front page changing the look and feel of the Moodle course. We learn how to make some changes to MoodleCloud, taking into account its limitations. There are customizable areas, though.

`Chapter 5`, *Customizing Elements with CSS*, works with several online text editors so as to learn more about CSS and what we can do in order to change the look and feel of Moodle on-premises. We test the code before making any changes and avoid making mistakes when customizing the look and feel of the Moodle theme.

`Chapter 6`, *Locating, Editing, and Using New Icons*, works with icons, vector graphics, and bitmaps. We learn who to modify SVG and export them as PNG. We change the look and feel of the Moodle on-premises course and personalize the icon. We can also add more images to the icons or edit them in a different way, but we always have to follow the steps that we have taken. We need to make copies of files and replace the edited files with the originals. We may not like how the new icon looks in the Moodle course.

`Chapter 7`, *Optimizing Themes for Mobile Devices*, works with emulators for mobile devices; we also check Internet connectivity and learn how to modify, edit, and custom some of these options. We work with Google DevTools, which is an online emulator, and we can easily learn how to work with a mobile device from either our desktop or laptop. Moreover, we emulate network connectivity to check how the theme download in a mobile device. We can customize not only the device, but also its connectivity. Besides, when throttling the connectivity, we can see the speed.

`Chapter 8`, *Exploring Layouts*, deals with all the themes available for Moodle 3.1 and Moodle 3, which are free of charge and downloadable at `https://moodle.org/plugins/browse.ph p?list=category&id=3`. We change the look and feel of our Moodle course several times in order to show how it looks dressed in other themes.

`Chapter 9`, *Course Formats*, deals with course formats. There are default course formats and there is also a plugin for them. These course formats can be downloaded from the Moodle website and can be installed in Moodle on-premises. We can also change the format of our courses in order to enhance them and make them a little bit different. We have to bear in mind what type of course we need to create in order to choose the right format.

`Chapter 10`, *Extending Moodle Theming to Specific Sections*, combines all the elements that we have learned throughout the chapters. We also add some ingredients in some cases that allow us to change the appearance of the Moodle course in order to customize it in the desired way.

Furthermore, we explore different ways in which we can simply change the look and feel of the course, since we can add just blocks, images, or make some small changes to the Moodle course that will allow us to see it in a different way.

Whenever we design an activity or add a resource, we must also bear in mind that we need to think how to organize them, due to the fact that the course will look tidier depending on how we organize the content.

What you need for this book

As requirements or prerequisites, readers need previous basic experience with Moodle 3 or earlier versions.

Who this book is for

If you are a Moodle administrator, developer, or designer and wish to enhance your Moodle site to make it visually attractive, then this book is for you. You should be familiar with basic web design techniques such as HTML and further experience with CSS would be helpful.

Conventions

In this book, you will find a number of text styles that distinguish between different kinds of information. Here are some examples of these styles and an explanation of their meaning.

Code words in text, database table names, folder names, filenames, file extensions, pathnames, dummy URLs, user input, and Twitter handles are shown as follows: "Change the number of pixels for the second element (image). Change from 120px (120 pixels) to 80px for both height and width."

A block of code is set as follows:

```
<!DOCTYPE html>
    <html>
    <head>
    <style>
    div {
        width: 500px;
        height: 100px;
        border: 3px solid #73AD21;
    }
```

New terms and **important words** are shown in bold. Words that you see on the screen, for example, in menus or dialog boxes, appear in the text like this: "We click on **Add an activity or resource** and two options appear, **resources** and **activities**."

Warnings or important notes appear in a box like this.

Tips and tricks appear like this.

Reader feedback

Feedback from our readers is always welcome. Let us know what you think about this book-what you liked or disliked. Reader feedback is important for us as it helps us develop titles that you will really get the most out of. To send us general feedback, simply e-mail `feedback@packtpub.com`, and mention the book's title in the subject of your message. If there is a topic that you have expertise in and you are interested in either writing or contributing to a book, see our author guide at `www.packtpub.com/authors`.

Customer support

Now that you are the proud owner of a Packt book, we have a number of things to help you to get the most from your purchase.

Errata

Although we have taken every care to ensure the accuracy of our content, mistakes do happen. If you find a mistake in one of our books-maybe a mistake in the text or the code-we would be grateful if you could report this to us. By doing so, you can save other readers from frustration and help us improve subsequent versions of this book. If you find any errata, please report them by visiting `http://www.packtpub.com/submit-errata`, selecting your book, clicking on the **Errata Submission Form** link, and entering the details of your errata. Once your errata are verified, your submission will be accepted and the errata will be uploaded to our website or added to any list of existing errata under the Errata section of that title.

To view the previously submitted errata, go to `https://www.packtpub.com/books/content/support` and enter the name of the book in the search field. The required information will appear under the **Errata** section.

Piracy

Piracy of copyrighted material on the Internet is an ongoing problem across all media. At Packt, we take the protection of our copyright and licenses very seriously. If you come across any illegal copies of our works in any form on the Internet, please provide us with the location address or website name immediately so that we can pursue a remedy.

Please contact us at `copyright@packtpub.com` with a link to the suspected pirated material.

We appreciate your help in protecting our authors and our ability to bring you valuable content.

Questions

If you have a problem with any aspect of this book, you can contact us at `questions@packtpub.com`, and we will do our best to address the problem.

1
An Introduction to Moodle 3 and MoodleCloud

In this chapter, we will introduce e-learning and virtual learning environments: Moodle and **MoodleCloud**, explaining their similarities and differences. Apart from that, we will learn and understand screen resolution and aspect ratio, which is the information we need in order to develop Moodle themes in the next chapters. We will also cover sizing the screen resolution, aspect ratio, and use Moodle in different types of devices. Furthermore, we will also deal with images and text. So, in this chapter, we shall learn the following topics:

- Understanding what e-learning is
- Learning about virtual learning environments
- Introducing Moodle and MoodleCloud
- Learning what Moodle and MoodleCloud are
- Using Moodle on different devices
- Sizing the screen resolution
- Calculating the aspect ratio
- Learning about sharp and soft images
- Learning about crisp and sharp text
- Understanding what anti-aliasing is

Understanding what e-learning is

E-learning is electronic learning, meaning that it is not traditional learning in a classroom with a teacher and students, plus the board. e-learning involves using a computer to deliver classes or a course.

When delivering classes or a course, there is an online interaction between the student and the teacher. There might also be some offline activities when a student is asked to create a piece of writing or something else. Another option is that there are collaboration activities involving the interaction of several students and the teacher.

When creating course content, there is the option of video conferencing as well. So there is virtual face-to-face interaction within the e-learning process. The time and the date should be set beforehand. In this way, e-learning is trying to imitate traditional learning to not lose human contact or social interaction.

The course may be full distance or not. If the course is full distance, there is online interaction only. All the resources and activities are delivered online and there might be some interaction through messages, chats, or e-mails between the student and the teacher.

If the course is not full distance and is delivered face to face but involving the use of computers, we are referring to blended learning. Blended learning means using e-learning within the classroom, and is a mixture of traditional learning and computers.

The use of blended learning with little children is very important because they get the social element, which is essential at a very young age. Apart from that, they also come into contact with technology while they are learning. It is advisable to use **Interactive Whiteboards (IWBs)** at an early stage.

IWBs are the right tool to choose when dealing with blended learning. IWBs are motivational gadgets, which are prominent in integrating technology into the classroom. IWBs are considered a symbol of innovation and a key element of teaching students.

IWBs offer interactive projections for class demonstrations; we can usually project resources from computer software as well as from our Moodle platform. Students can interact with them by touching or writing on them, that is to say, through blended learning. Apart from that, teachers can make presentations on different topics within a subject and these topics become much more interesting and captivating for students, since IWBs allow changes to be made in the interactive elements and we can insert those into the presentation of any subject. There are several types of technology used in IWBs, such as touch technology, laser scanning, and electromagnetic writing tools. Therefore, we have to bear in mind which to choose when we get an IWB.

On the other hand, the widespread use of mobile devices nowadays has turned e-learning into mobile learning. Smartphones and tablets allow students to learn anywhere at any time. Therefore, it is important to design course material that is usable by students on such devices.

Moodle is a learning platform through which we can design, build, and create e-learning environments. It is possible to create online interaction and have video conferencing sessions with students. Distance learning is another option if blended learning cannot be carried out.

We can also choose Moodle mobile. We can download the app from the App Store, Google Play, Windows Store, or Windows Phone Store. We can browse the content of courses, receive messages, contact people from the courses, upload different types of file, and view course grades, among other actions.

Learning about Virtual Learning Environments

A **Virtual Learning Environment** (**VLE**) is a type of virtual environment that supports both resources and learning activities; therefore, students can have both passive and active roles. There is also social interaction, which can take place through collaborative work as well as video conferencing. Students can also be actors since they can also construct the VLE.

VLEs can be used for both distance and blended learning since they can enrich courses. Mobile learning is also possible because mobile devices have access to the Internet, allowing teachers and students to log in to their courses.

VLEs are designed in such a way that they can carry out the following functions or activities:

- Design, create, store, access, and use course content
- Deliver or share course content
- Communicate, interact, and collaborate with students and teachers
- Assess and personalize the learning experience
- Modularize both activities and resources
- Customize the interface

We are going to deal with each of these functions and activities and see how useful they might be when designing our VLE for our class. When using Moodle, we can perform all the functions and activities mentioned here, because Moodle is a VLE.

Designing, creating, storing, accessing, and using course content

If we use the Moodle platform to create the course, we have to deal with course content. Therefore, when we add a course, we have to add its content. We can choose the weekly outline section or the topic under which we want to add the content. We click on **Add an activity or** resource and two options appear, **resources** and **activities**; therefore, the content can be passive or active for the student. When we create or design activities in Moodle, the options are shown in the following screenshot:

Another option for creating course content is to reuse content that has already been created and used before in another VLE. In other words, we can import or export course materials, since most VLEs have specific tools designed for such purposes. This is very useful and saves time.

There are a variety of ways for teachers to create course materials, due to the fact that the teacher thinks of the methodology, as well as how to meet the student's needs when creating the course. Moodle is designed in such a way that it offers a variety of combinations that can fit any course content.

Delivering or sharing course content

Before using VLEs, we have to log in, because all the content is protected and is not open to the general public. In this way, we can protect property rights, as well as the course itself. All participants must be enrolled in the course unless it has been opened to the public.

Teachers can gain remote access in order to create and design their courses. This is quite profitable since they can build the content at home, rather than in their workplace. They need login access and they need to switch roles to course creator in order to create the content. Follow this to switch roles to course creator:

Under **Administration**, click on **Switch role to...** | **Course creator**, as shown in the following screenshot:

When the role has been changed, the teacher can create content that students can access. Once logged in, students have access to the already created content, either activities or resources. The content is available over the Internet or the institution's intranet connection. Students can access the content anywhere if any of these connections are available.

If MoodleCloud is being used, there must be an Internet connection, otherwise it is impossible for both students and teachers to log in.

Communicating, interacting, and collaborating with students and teachers

Communication, interaction, and collaborative working are the key factors to social interaction and learning through interchanging ideas. VLEs let us create course content activities, because these actions give our class a social element. There is no need to be an isolated learner, because learners have the ability to communicate between themselves and with the teachers.

Moodle offers the possibility of video conferencing through the Big Blue Button. In order to install the Big Blue Button plugin in Moodle, visit the following link: `https://moodle.org /plugins/browse.php?list=set&id=2`. This is shown in the following screenshot:

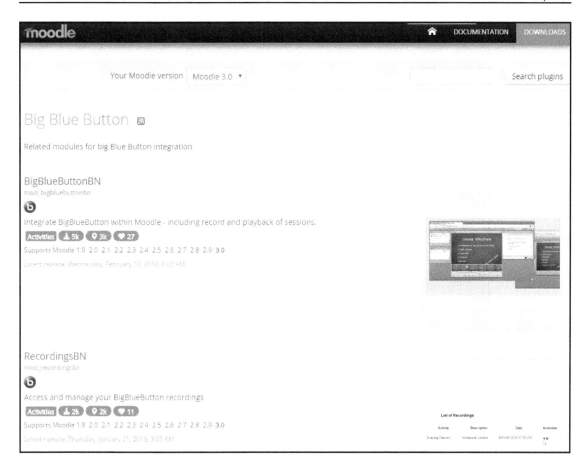

If you are using MoodleCloud, the Big Blue Button is enabled by default, so when we click on **Add an activity or resource**, it appears in the list of activities, as shown in the following screenshot:

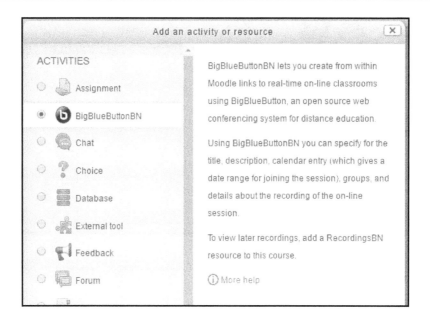

Assessing and personalizing the learning experience

Moodle allows the teacher to follow the progress of students so that they can assess and grade their work, as long as they complete the activities. Resources cannot be graded, since they are passive content for students, but teachers can also check when a participant last accessed the site.

Badges are another element used to personalize the learning experience. We can create badges for students when they complete an activity or a course; they are homework rewards. Badges are quite good at motivating young learners.

Modularizing both activities and resources

Moodle offers the ability to build personalized activities and resources. There are several ways to present both, with all the options Moodle offers. Activities can be molded according to the methodology the teacher uses.

In Moodle 3, there are new question types within the **Quiz** activity. The question types are as follows:

- **Select missing words**
- **Drag and drop into text**
- **Drag and drop onto image**
- **Drag and drop markers**

The question types are shown after we choose **Quiz** in the **Add an activity or resource** menu, in the weekly outline section or topic that we have chosen. The types of question are shown in the following screenshot:

Customizing the interface

Moodle allows us to customize the interface in order to develop the look and feel that we require; we can add a logo for the school or institution that the Moodle site belongs to.

We can also add another theme relevant to the subject or course that we have created. The main purpose in customizing the interface is to avoid all subjects and courses looking the same. Later in the chapter, we will learn how to customize the interface.

Learning Moodle and MoodleCloud

Modular Object-Oriented Dynamic Learning Environment (**Moodle**) is a learning platform designed in such a way that we can create VLEs. Moodle can be downloaded, installed and run on any web server software using **Hypertext Preprocessor** (**PHP**). It can support a SQL database and can run on several operating systems. We can download Moodle 3.0.3 (the latest version at the time of writing this book) from the following URL: `ht tps://download.moodle.org/`. This URL is shown in the following screenshot:

MoodleCloud, on the other hand, does not need to be downloaded since, as its name suggests, is in the cloud. Therefore, we can get our own Moodle site with MoodleCloud within minutes and for free. It is Moodle's hosting platform, designed and run by the people who make Moodle. In order to get a MoodleCloud site, we need to go to the following URL: `https://moodle.com/cloud/`. This is shown in the following screenshot:

MoodleCloud was created in order to cater for users with fewer requirements and small budgets. In order to create an account, you need to add your cell phone number to receive an SMS which we must be input when creating your site.

As it is free, there are some limitations to MoodleCloud, unless we contact Moodle Partners and pay for an expanded version of it. The limitations are as follows:

- No more than 50 users
- 200 MB disk space
- Core themes and plugins only
- One site per phone number
- Big Blue Button sessions are limited to six people, with no recordings
- There are advertisements

There is another option for MoodleCloud which is paid and grants more benefits, but throughout the book, we will deal with the free version of MoodleCloud.

When creating a Moodle site, we want to change the look and functionality of the site or individual course. We may also need to customize themes for Moodle, in order to give the course the desired look.

Therefore, this chapter will explain the basic concepts that we have to bear in mind when dealing with themes, due to the fact that themes are shown in different devices. In the past, Moodle ran only on desktops or laptops, but nowadays Moodle can run on many different devices, such as smartphones, tablets, iPads, and smart TVs, and the list goes on.

Using Moodle on different devices

Moodle can be used on different devices, at different times, in different places. Therefore, there are factors that we need to be aware of when designing courses and themes.

Therefore, hereafter in this chapter, there are several aspects and concepts that we need to look into in more detail in order to understand what we need to take into account when we design our courses and build our themes.

Devices change in many ways, not only in size but also in the way they display our Moodle course. Moodle courses can be used on anything from a tiny device that fits into the palm of a hand to a huge IWB or smart TV, and plenty of other devices in between. Therefore, such differences have to be taken into account when choosing images, text, and other components of our course.

We are going to deal with sizing screen resolution, calculating the aspect ratio, types of images such as sharp and soft, and crisp and sharp text. Finally, but importantly, the anti-aliasing method is explained.

Sizing the screen resolution

A number of pixels the display of device has, horizontally and vertically, and the color depth measuring the number of bits representing the color of each pixel makes up the screen resolution. The higher the screen resolution, the higher the productivity we get.

In the past, the screen resolution of a display was important since it determined the amount of information displayed on the screen. The lower the resolution, the fewer items would fit on the screen; the higher the resolution, the more items would fit on the screen. The resolution varies according to the hardware in each device.

Nowadays, the screen resolution is considered a pleasant visual experience, since we would rather see more quality than more stuff on the screen. That is the reason why the screen resolution matters. There might be different display sizes where the screen resolutions are the same, that is to say, the total number of pixels is the same. If we compare a laptop (13" screen with a resolution of 1280 x 800) and a desktop (with a 17" monitor with the same 1280 x 800 resolution), although the monitor is larger, the number of pixels is the same; the only difference is that we will be able to see everything bigger on the monitor. Therefore, instead of seeing more stuff, we see higher quality.

Screen resolution chart

Code	Width	Height	Ratio	Description
QVGA	320	240	4:3	Quarter Video Graphics Array
FHD	1920	1080	~16:9	Full High Definition
HVGA	640	240	8:3	Half Video Graphics Array
HD	1360	768	~16:9	High Definition
HD	1366	768	~16:9	High Definition
HD+	1600	900	~16:9	High Definition plus
VGA	640	480	4:3	Video Graphics Array
SVGA	800	600	4:3	Super Video Graphics Array
XGA	1024	768	4:3	Extended Graphics Array
XGA+	1152	768	3:2	Extended Graphics Array plus
XGA+	1152	864	4:3	Extended Graphics Array plus
SXGA	1280	1024	5:4	Super Extended Graphics Array
SXGA+	1400	1050	4:3	Super Extended Graphics Array plus
UXGA	1600	1200	4:3	Ultra Extended Graphics Array
QXGA	2048	1536	4:3	Quad Extended Graphics Array

WXGA	1280	768	5:3	Wide Extended Graphics Array
WXGA	1280	720	~16:9	Wide Extended Graphics Array
WXGA	1280	800	16:10	Wide Extended Graphics Array
WXGA	1366	768	~16:9	Wide Extended Graphics Array
WXGA+	1280	854	3:2	Wide Extended Graphics Array plus
WXGA+	1440	900	16:10	Wide Extended Graphics Array plus
WXGA+	1440	960	3:2	Wide Extended Graphics Array plus
WQHD	2560	1440	~16:9	Wide Quad High Definition
WQXGA	2560	1600	16:10	Wide Quad Extended Graphics Array
WSVGA	1024	600	~17:10	Wide Super Video Graphics Array
WSXGA	1600	900	~16:9	Wide Super Extended Graphics Array
WSXGA	1600	1024	16:10	Wide Super Extended Graphics Array
WSXGA+	1680	1050	16:10	Wide Super Extended Graphics Array plus
WUXGA	1920	1200	16:10	Wide Ultra Extended Graphics Array
WQXGA	2560	1600	16:10	Wide Quad Extended Graphics Array
WQUXGA	3840	2400	16:10	Wide Quad Ultra Extended Graphics Array
4K UHD	3840	2160	16:9	Ultra High Definition
4K UHD	1536	864	16:9	Ultra High Definition

Considering that 3840 x 2160 displays (also known as 4K, QFHD, Ultra HD, UHD, or 2160p) are already available for laptops and monitors, a pleasant visual experience with high DPI displays can be a good long-term investment for your desktop applications.

The DPI setting for the monitor causes another common problem: the change in the effective resolution. Consider the 13.3" display that offers a 3200 x1800 resolution and is configured with an OS DPI of 240 DPI. The high DPI setting makes the system use both larger fonts and UI elements; therefore, the elements consume more pixels to render than the same elements displayed in the resolution configured with an OS DPI of 96 DPI. The effective resolution of a display that provides 3200 x1800 pixels configured at 240 DPI is 1280 x 720. The effective resolution can become a big problem because an application that requires a minimum resolution of the old standard 1024 x 768 pixels with an OS DPI of 96 would have problems with a 3200 x 1800-pixel display configured at 240 DPI, and it wouldn't be possible to display all the necessary UI elements. It may sound crazy, but the effective vertical resolution is 720 pixels, lower than the 768 vertical pixels required by the application to display all the UI elements without problems.

The formula to calculate the effective resolution is simple: divide the physical pixels by the scale factor (OS DPI / 96). For example, the following formula calculates the horizontal effective resolution of my previous example: 3200 / (240 / 96) = 3200 / 2.5 = 1280; and the following formula calculates the vertical effective resolution: 1800 / (240 / 96) = 1800 / 2.5 = 720.

The effective resolution would be of 1800 x 900 pixels if the same physical resolution were configured at 192 DPI. Effective horizontal resolution: 3200 / (192 / 96) = 3200 / 2 = 1600; and vertical effective resolution: 1800 / (192 / 96) = 1800 / 2 = 900.

Calculating the aspect ratio

The aspect radio is the proportional relationship between the width and the height of an image. It is used to describe the shape of a computer screen or a TV. The aspect ratio of a standard-definition (SD) screen is 4:3, that is to say, a relatively square rectangle. The aspect ratio is often expressed in W:H format, where W stands for width and H stands for height. 4:3 means four units wide to three units high. With regards to high-definition TV (HDTV), they have a 16:9 ratio, which is a wider rectangle.

Why do we calculate the aspect ratio? The answer to this question is that the ratio has to be well defined because the rectangular shape that every frame, digital video, canvas, image, or responsive design has, makes shapes fit into different and distinct devices.

Learning about sharp and soft images

Images can be either sharp or soft. Sharp is the opposite of soft. A soft image has less pronounced details, while a sharp image has more contrast between pixels. The more pixels the image has, the sharper it is. We can soften the image, in which case it loses information, but we cannot sharpen one; in other words, we can't add more information to an image.

In order to compare sharp and soft images, we can visit the following website, where we can convert bitmaps to vector graphics. We can convert a bitmap images such as `.png`, `.jpeg`, or `.gif` into a `.svg` in order to get an anti-aliased image. We can do this with a simple step. We work with an online tool to vectorize the bitmap using `http://vectormagi c.com/home`. There are plenty of features to take into account when vectorizing.

We can design a bitmap using an image editor and upload the bitmap image from the clipboard, or upload the file from our computer. Once the image is uploaded to the application, we can start working. Another possibility is to use the sample images on the website, which we are going to use in order to see that anti-aliasing effect.

We convert bitmap images, which are made up of pixels, into vector images, which are made up of shapes. The shapes are mathematical descriptions of images and do not become pixelated when scaling up. Vector graphics can handle scaling without any problems. Vector images are the preferred type to work with in graphic design on paper or clothes.

Go to `http://vectormagic.com/home` and click on **Examples**, as shown in the following screenshot:

After clicking on **Examples**, the bitmap appears on the left and the vectorized image on the right. The bitmap is blurred and soft; the SVG has an anti-aliasing effect, therefore the image is sharp. The result is shown in the following screenshot:

Learning about crisp and sharp text

There are sharp and soft images, and there is also crisp and sharp text, so it is now time to look at text. What is the main difference between these two? When we say that the text is crisp, we mean that there is more anti-aliasing, in other words it has more grey pixels around the black text. The difference is shown when we zoom in to 400%. On the other hand, sharp mode is superior for small fonts because it makes each letter stronger.

There are four options in Photoshop to deal with text: sharp, crisp, strong, and smooth. Sharp and crisp have already been mentioned in the previous paragraphs. Strong is notorious for adding unnecessary weight to letter forms, and smooth looks closest to the untinted anti-aliasing, and it remains similar to the original.

The following screenshot displays crisp text:

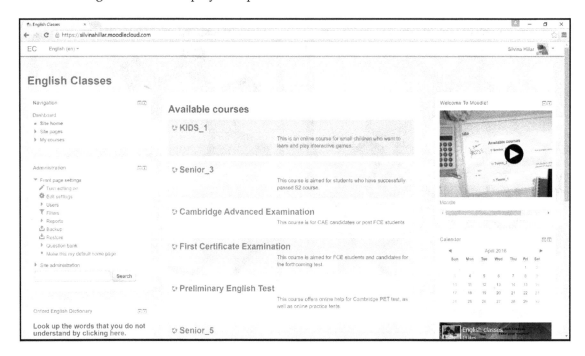

Windows 10, high-dpi screen, 3200 x 1800 resolution, also known as WQXGA+, landscape view.

Another example of crisp text is the following:

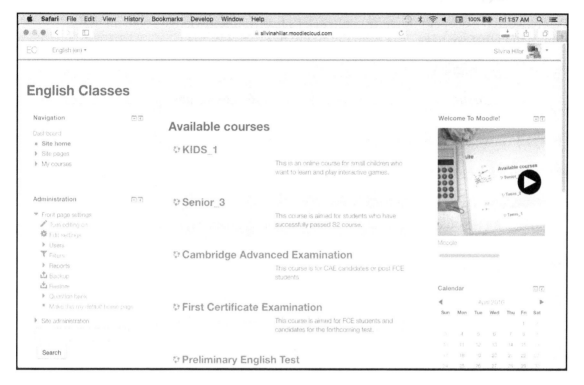

High-dpi retina display on OS X, Safari, 2560 x 1600.

Understanding what anti-aliasing is

The word anti-aliasing means the technique used in order to minimize the distortion artifacts. It applies intermediate colors in order to eliminate pixels, that is to say the saw-tooth or pixelated lines. Therefore, we need to look at a lower resolution so that the saw-tooth effect does not appear when we make the graphic bigger.

Test your knowledge

Before we delve deeper into more content, let's test your knowledge about all the information that we have dealt with in this chapter:

A. Moodle is a learning platform with which …

1. …we can design, build and create e-learning environments.
2. …we can learn.
3. …we can download content for students.

B. BigBlueButtonBN …

1. …is a way to log in to Moodle.
2. …lets you create links to real-time online classrooms from within Moodle.
3. …works only in MoodleCloud.

C. MoodleCloud …

1. …is not open source.
2. …does not allow more than 50 users.
3. …works only for universities.

D. The number of pixels the display of the device has horizontally and vertically, and the color depth measuring the number of bits representing the color of each pixel, make up …

1. …screen resolution.
2. …aspect ratio.
3. …the size of a device.

E. Anti-aliasing can be applied to …

1. …only text.
2. …only images.
3. …both images and text.

Summary

In summary, in this first chapter, we have covered most of what needs to be known about e-learning, VLEs, and Moodle and MoodleCloud. There is a slight difference between Moodle and MoodleCloud especially if you don't have access to a Moodle course in the institution where you are working and want to design a Moodle course. Moodle is used in different devices and there are several aspects to take into account when designing a course and building a Moodle theme, which will be covered in the following chapters.

We have dealt with screen resolution, aspect ratio, types of images and text, and anti-aliasing effects.

In the next chapter, we will cover the basics of Moodle theming, including theme types, priority, the location of the theme directory, and the concept of parent themes. We will also cover browsing and changing a theme within Moodle and MoodleCloud, and search for, downloading, and installing custom themes. We will cover how to do these in different OSes, including Mac, Windows, and Android. We will then finish off by changing the theme settings in the Moodle theme settings page, both in Moodle and MoodleCloud.

2

Themes in Moodle 3 on-premises and MoodleCloud

In this chapter, we will cover the main aspects of Moodle theming of both Moodle and MoodleCloud. We will also change a theme, browse, select, and download it. We will also list the available themes in Moodle 3 on-premises at the time of the writing. We will work and understand how the Moodle theme More works with HTML tags. Afterwards, we will install the chosen theme. We can also create our themes from scratch in later chapters of the book, therefore it is necessary to understand what a theme is and how to change them. We shall learn the following topics in this chapter:

- Understanding what a Moodle theme is
- Learning about Moodle themes in MoodleCloud
- Using HTML tags to define colors
- Customizing Moodle or MoodleCloud's theme More using HTML to define colors
- Understanding types of Moodle and MoodleCloud themes
- Locating Moodle theme directory
- Selecting and download a Moodle theme for Moodle 3 on-premises
- Installing a Moodle theme

Understanding what a Moodle theme is

In order to work and deal with Moodle themes, we need to have access to the server, if we are to have Moodle 3 on-premises and are not using MoodleCloud hosted services. In the event that we want to change Moodle themes in MoodleCloud, we need to have access as an administrator. An important element to take into account is that when we need to change the themes in MoodleCloud, there happens to be more restrictions than when dealing with an already installed Moodle platform.

A Moodle theme changes the look and feel of Moodle, that is to say, it is a template that controls the way Moodle looks. An administrator can change Moodle themes through the administrative interface of Moodle. The theme does not change Moodle but it changes the way it looks. It can be useful to change the look of a Moodle site according to the place that the Moodle course is being used, not only just to see it in a different way but also in order to cope with the place that it represents.

In order to change Moodle themes, there are places where we can download themes for our Moodle course and we can also create a Moodle theme from scratch. In this chapter, we are going to deal with Moodle themes available for Moodle 3 on-premises at the time of writing; in the further chapters, we will design themes from scratch.

For web developers, there is a slight difference between theming and skinning. Theming is global and skinning is per control or element. Theming concerns all the settings and skinning deals with changing how controls look. But, said the definition is not per se like that due to the fact that theming is used in general and theming applies skins.

Therefore, we choose a theme and that theme can make it so that the windows are shown the same in Mac OS X or Windows. The choice between Mac OS X or Windows for the windows is skinning. On the other hand, the images, and their position on the screen, and the way content is distributed, including colors, is theming.

That is to say, once the theme is chosen, we can apply different skins, although, in Moodle, we refer to theming without making such division whatsoever. As these terms refer to the design (look and feel) rather than the functionality of the application.

As regards Moodle themes, we have two choices because we are dealing with both MoodleCloud and Moodle 3 on-premises as regards MoodleCloud, we can choose among four themes at the time of the writing; there is also the possibility to design your own Moodle theme.

On the other hand, in Moodle 3 on-premises we can choose among several themes. We can find free themes in the following website: `https://moodle.org/plugins/browse.php?list=category&id=3`. According to the Moodle version that we are dealing with is the Moodle theme that we can download. So, we enter the aforementioned website and we can find several Moodle themes, as shown in the following screenshot:

The previous screenshot shows two Moodle themes; there are more if you scroll down the website. There is a line that reads **Supports Moodle** and the Moodle versions appear there. The **Essential** theme supports Moodle 3 on-premises among other Moodle versions; on the other hand, **BCU** does not support Moodle 3 on-premises although it works with other Moodle versions.

So, in this website we can find free Moodle themes to download and install in our Moodle course. There are some websites which sell Moodle themes, which might be another choice if we are willing to pay for such themes. So there are two options; free themes or paid themes.

First, we will deal with MoodleCloud and afterwards we will deal with the Moodle platform. We will also cover how to change themes in different OSes such as Windows, Mac, and Android, both for desktop and mobile devices. There is also an option within themes that we have to take into account, that is, to allow it for mobile devices. Furthermore, different browsers are also necessary when dealing with themes. These topics will be dealt in this chapter and throughout the book.

Learning about Moodle themes in MoodleCloud

Moodle themes are part of Moodle plugins but MoodleCloud does not support plugins, therefore, as it has already been mentioned before, themes in MoodleCloud are limited. As a default, MoodleCloud has the More theme, as stated in the MoodleCloud website: `https ://moodle.com/cloud/faq/`, and it is shown in the following screenshot:

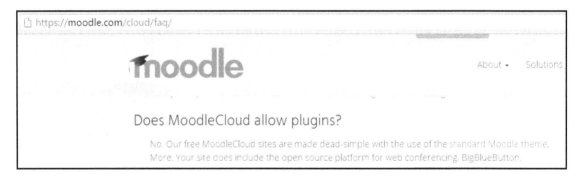

In order to change the MoodleCloud theme in a simple way, we can follow these steps:

1. Click on **Turn editing on**.
2. Click on **Site administration** | **Appearance** | **Themes** | **Theme selector**. The current theme of our MoodleCloud course appears, as shown in the following screenshot:

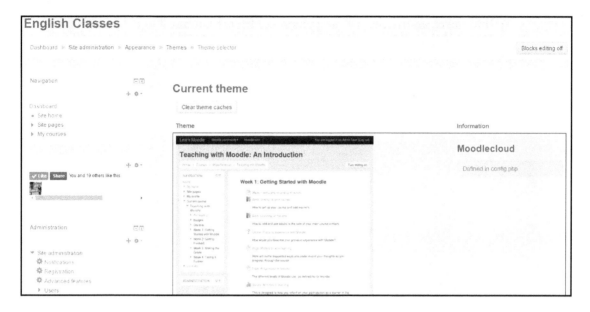

3. The current theme of our MoodleCloud course is set by default. In order to change the theme of our MoodleCloud course in a simple way, click on **Clean** on the left-hand side margin, as shown in the following screenshot:

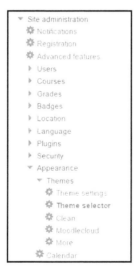

4. Within the clean theme, we can customize **Invert navbar**, **Logo**, **Custom CSS**, and **Footnote**, but we are not customizing them right now, so click on **Save changes**, as shown in the following screenshot:

5. After changing the theme, in this case in a very simple way without any customization whatsoever, the MoodleCloud course looks as shown in the following screenshot:

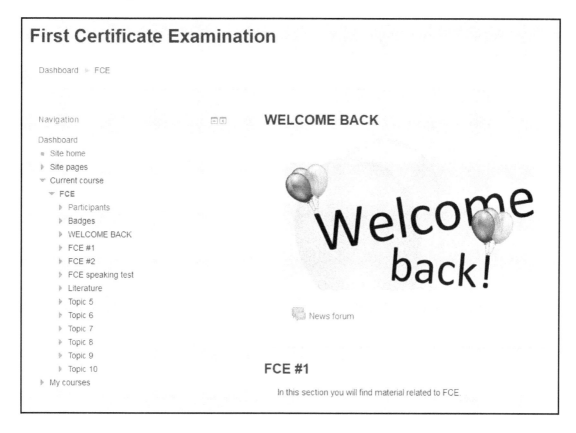

There are slight changes since the letters are in a slightly different color and blocks are gray instead of white, so we have successfully changed the theme of our MoodleCloud course.

Using HTML tags to define colors

HTML is found on all those pages that we find on the Internet. What we see on the screen has HTML code behind it. It also includes font colors, therefore we can change the color of text using HTML tags.

HTML tags are a bit complex. But we do not need to master the HTML standard in order to change colors. We can change colors using HTML code in a simple way. We can use a dynamic HTML color-code chart or an HTML code picker, such as the ones offered by the **HTML Color Codes** website: `http://html-color-codes.info/`.

We can click on one of the color boxes in the chart and the site will display the selected color code, as shown in the following screenshot:

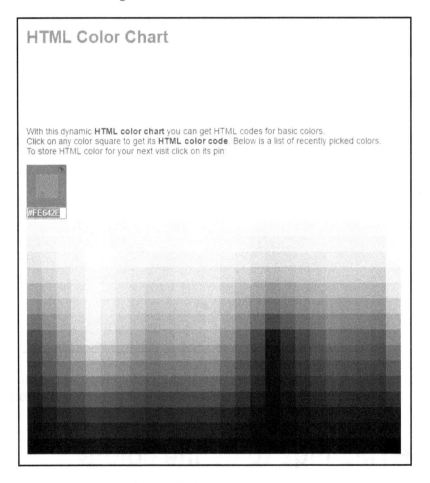

In this case, the selected color code is **#FE642E**. HTML codes define a color using a symbol (#) and a group of three two-digit hexadecimal numbers. Thus, we will see the # followed by six letters (A-F) or numbers (0-9). The three two-digit hexadecimal numbers represent the intensity of the red, green, and blue colors. When combining the intensity of red, green, and blue, you can produce millions of different colors.

We can also move a vertical slider to choose the hue and then click on the color square in the HTML Color Picker and the site will display the selected color code, as shown in the following screenshot:

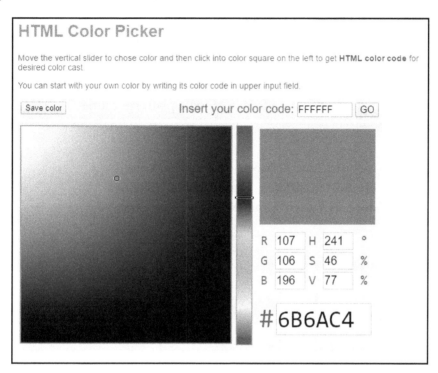

Why do we need all this information about the HTML tags? The answer is very simple. We need information about the HTML tags because we can define background colors in our Moodle course. When we do not want to use the default background colors, we can edit HTML code to specify different background colors using the MoodleCloud theme More and edit HTML code as simply as we have just done using the HTML Code Chart or HTML Color Picker.

Customizing Moodle or MoodleCloud's theme More using HTML to define colors

More is a customizable theme which makes it easy to choose the desired colors for the MoodleCloud or Moodle platform course. Another important asset about this theme is that if you do not know how to create or develop a theme from scratch, More allows us to choose different colors.

In this case, we are customizing More from a Moodle platform course. The steps are the same for MoodleCloud. There are some steps that we have to follow in order to customize More:

1. Enter the MoodleCloud or Moodle platform course.
2. Click on **Site Administration** | **Appearance** | **Themes**.
3. Click on **More**, as shown in the following screenshot:

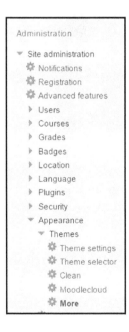

4. When we click on **More,** the HTML code charts appear, as shown in the following screenshot:

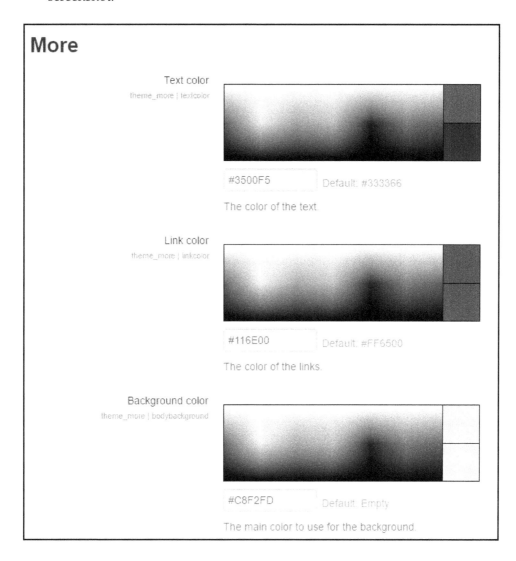

5. We can change colors by using a kind of HTML code chart, which was previously explained in the *Using HTML tags to define colors* section. The following screenshot shows how we can change the text color by just clicking on the desired color:

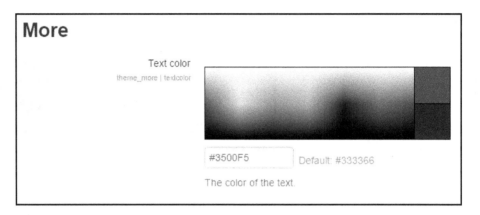

6. The chosen **Text color** generated the following HTML code: #3500F5, as previously explained.
7. Click on the other HTML code charts in order to change the **Link color** and the **Background color**. The chosen codes are shown in the following screenshot:

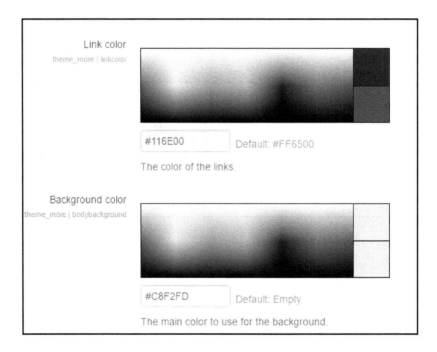

8. There are more features that we can customize within the More theme; bear in mind that it is tough to develop our MoodleCloud or Moodle platform theme so as to avoid creating a theme from scratch. So far, scroll down the page and click on **Save changes**, as shown in the following screenshot:

9. Our Moodle platform course looks as shown in the following screenshot:

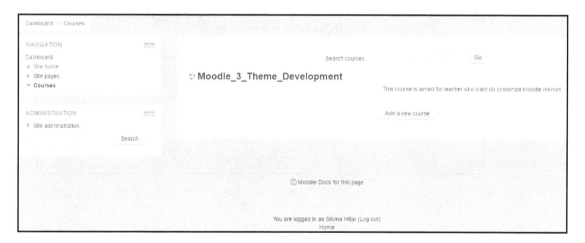

Remember to click on **Theme Designer Mode** within **Theme settings** before changing themes in our Moodle platform course or MoodleCloud. Follow these steps:

1. Under **Site administration** click on **Appearance** | **Themes** | **Theme settings**. As shown in the following screenshot:

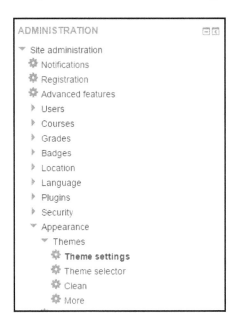

2. Within **Theme settings**, click on **Theme designer mode**, as shown in the following screenshot:

Understanding types of Moodle and MoodleCloud themes

We can customize Moodle themes within **Theme settings** so that they are assigned to different contexts such as site, users, courses, and categories. Therefore, we can have one site theme but we can choose a different course or category theme. We just have to customize the settings in order to allow it and make it possible.

User themes

Users can choose their preferred theme on the Edit profile page. All the Moodle pages will show the theme which has been chosen by the user. in order to enable a user to change the theme, we must click on **Allow user themes** within **Site Administration | Appearance | Themes | Theme settings**. Click on **Allow user themes**, as shown in the following screenshot:

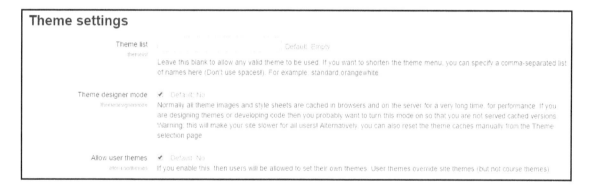

Then scroll down the page and click on **Save changes**.

Course themes

Any user with the proper permissions, including teachers with editing permissions, can change to the desired theme in order to design the course theme. Course theme overrides site themes, user themes, or session themes. In other words, if a user has set a theme and the editing teacher has set the course theme, the course theme is the one which is going to be seen instead of the one chosen by the user.

In order to allow an editing teacher to design a course theme, we must follow these steps:

1. Under **Site administration**, click on **Appearance** | **Themes** | **Theme selector**.
2. Click on **Allow course themes** as shown in the following screenshot:

Allow course themes	☑	Default: No
allowcoursethemes		If you enable this, then courses will be allowed to set their own themes. Course themes override all other theme choices (site, user, or session themes)

3. Then scroll down the page and click on **Save changes**.

Category themes

There is the option of choosing a theme by category. It is not advisable to work with it since there is a warning tip because it may affect performance. Category themes affect other course themes:

1. Under **Site administration**, click on **Appearance** | **Themes** | **Theme selector**.
2. Click on **Allow category themes** if you consider that it is necessary; otherwise, it is not advisable. It is shown in the following screenshot:

Allow category themes	☐	Default: No
Defined in config.php		If you enable this, then themes can be set at the category level. This will affect all child categories and courses
allowcategorythemes		unless they have specifically set their own theme. WARNING: Enabling category themes may affect performance.

3. Then scroll down the page and click on **Save changes**.

   When selecting another theme in order to be detected by different mobile devices, smartphones, desktops, and so on, we have to click on **Enable device detection**.

   Under Site administration, click on **Appearance** | **Themes** | **Theme settings**. Click on **Enable device detection**, as shown in the following screenshot:

4. Click on **Save changes**.

Locating the Moodle theme directory

The Moodle theme directory can be found at Local Disk `C:/Moodle30/server/moodle/theme`, as shown in the following screenshot:

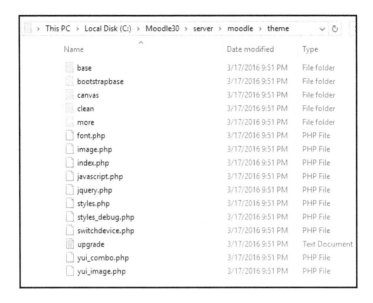

The directory has the following Moodle themes as standard: base, bootstrapbase, canvas, clean, and more. When we click on any of these Moodle themes, we can display a list of folders and files which are contained in the Moodle theme. For instance, in this case, we click on moodle | theme | more and these are the files and folders that we can find, as shown in the following screenshot:

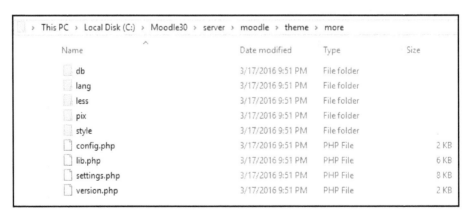

Each Moodle theme file and folder contains information and can be edited so as to customize Moodle themes. We will deal with these folders in later chapters; so far, we have learned where to locate Moodle themes and their folders.

Selecting and downloading a Moodle theme for Moodle 3 on-premises

We can download Moodle themes for our Moodle on-premises course, and we can do that from the following website: `https://moodle.org/plugins/browse.php?list=category&id=3`. We can look for a theme which is suitable for Moodle 3 on-premises; in this case, we are going to choose Essential, as shown in the following screenshot:

We click on **Essential** in order to be able to download the Moodle theme. The following screenshot appears, click on **Download** in order to download the theme, as shown in the following screenshot:

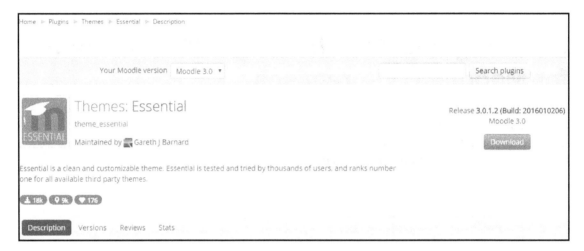

After downloading the theme, the file will appear within the Downloads folder, as shown in the following screenshot:

Installing a Moodle theme

We will learn how to install a Moodle theme in the following steps:

1. We have just downloaded Moodle theme essential. What we need to do is to install it in order to use it in our Moodle on-premises course. Therefore, we right-click on the Moodle theme file/folder and click on **Copy**, as shown in the following screenshot:

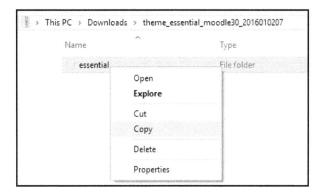

2. We have previously located our Moodle on-premises course directory and we need to go there in order to paste the file that we have already copied. Therefore, we go to Local Disk `C:/Moodle30/server/moodle/theme` and we right-click and click on **Paste**. The file takes some seconds to be pasted, as shown in the following screenshot:

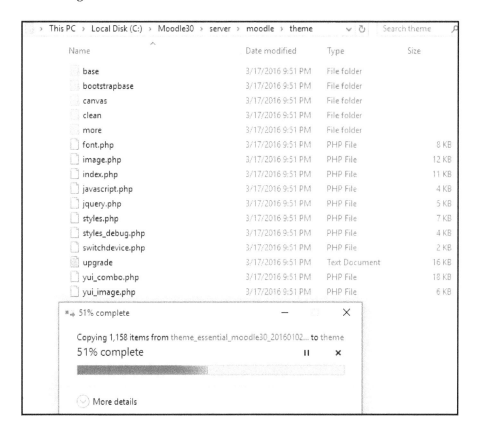

3. When the pasting has just finished, we can see the Moodle theme file displayed, as shown in the following screenshot:

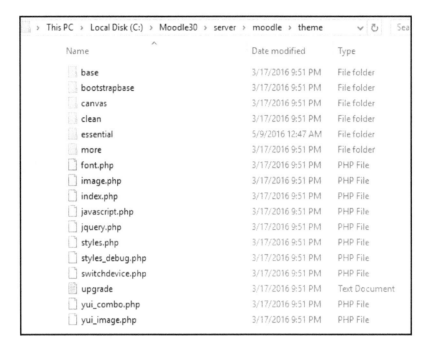

4. We enter our Moodle on-premises course and there is an upgrade of the database because we have already installed the Moodle theme Essential; therefore, the following screen appears, as shown in this screenshot:

5. Click on **Upgrade Moodle database now**. Then the following screen appears, showing that the plugins were successfully upgraded, as shown in the following screenshot:

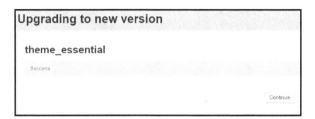

6. Click on **Continue**. The following screen appears showing the Essential Moodle theme which has been installed and upgraded. Therefore, we can customize this Moodle theme or leave it as it is and click on **Save changes** in order to use it as it was installed. In this case, we click on **Save changes**, as shown in the following screenshot:

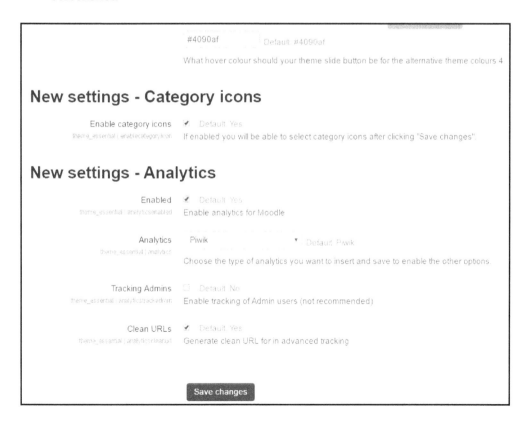

7. When we enter our Moodle on-premises, course we can choose the Moodle theme Essential as shown in the following screenshot:

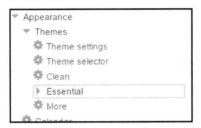

8. When we click on **Essential** the following drop-down menu appears, as shown in the following screenshot:

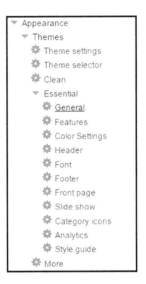

9. Each of the items displayed can be customized. Therefore, we click on each of them and customize them in the desired way. Later, we click on **Save changes** in order to change the theme in our Moodle on-premises course.

Test your knowledge

A. MoodleCloud offers …

1. …a restrictive number of themes because there are no plugins available.
2. …a great variety of themes which can be downloaded from moodle.org.
3. …free and open source themes as well as paid ones.

B. More theme can be customized …

1. …if we download a plugin.
2. …directly from our Moodle on-premises course or MoodleCloud course using HTML tags.
3. …if we create a theme from scratch.

C. Course themes …

1. …can't override user themes.
2. …overrides user themes.
3. …are designed by students.

D. The Essential Moodle theme can be …

1. …downloaded from `www.moodle.org` and customized.
2. …bought for a very low price.
3. …found in the Moodle directory.

E. Mobiles app can be detected only if …

1. …the themes are customized.
2. …we open our Moodle on-premises course on a mobile device.
3. …the **Enable device detection** icon is ticked within **Theme settings**.

Summary

In summary, in this second chapter, we have learned what themes are and how to find them in Moodle on-premises and in MoodleCloud. We have also learned a little about HTML code and how colors are named in this code. We also customized Moodle themes more and found out where our Moodle themes are on our computer. We have searched for, downloaded, and installed the Moodle theme Essential.

We have dealt with plenty of information relevant to Moodle themes and where to find them. In the following chapter, we will deal with logos, how to design them and add them to both MoodleCloud and Moodle on-premises. We will also learn how to download and change the Favicon to Moodle on-premises. Furthermore, we will add a header background image to Moodle on-premises. Let's keep theming!

3
Setting Up Logos in Moodle Themes

In this chapter, we will use the UI to cover how to design a logo for Moodle on-premises and MoodleCloud. We will use an online logo designer since it can be used on our computer or smartphone, and it works on different OSes. Logos are very important for a Moodle course since they represent the organization that we are working for. We need to upload an image to enhance the look and feel of our Moodle course.

We are also going to change the Favicon of the Moodle course so that all the logos are new and the look and feel changes. Therefore, we will learn how to do this with the Essential theme in Moodle on-premises. We will add a header background image to the Essential theme in a tiled style so that the image is repeated throughout the header.

In this chapter, we shall cover the following topics:

- Designing a logo
- Adding a logo to MoodleCloud in the More theme
- Adding a logo to the Essential theme in Moodle on-premises
- Downloading a Favicon
- Changing the Favicon in the Essential theme in Moodle on-premises
- Adding a header background image in the Essential theme in Moodle on-premises

Designing a logo

A logo is a representation of the place that we belong to or that we are working for. According to the Merriam-Webster dictionary, a logo is:

"A symbol that is used to identify a company and that appears on its products."

We can design a logo using an online logo maker. There are several options when designing a logo if you don't have one already. One option would be to use the following site: `http://www.onlinelogomaker.com/`. On this website, we can design a logo for free. One of the greatest advantages of websites such as online logo maker is that you can even create a logo on your smartphone or tablet. It also works with both Windows and iOSx.

In order to create a logo, there are some steps that we have to follow. These are the steps:

1. Go to `http://www.onlinelogomaker.com/`, as shown in the following screenshot:

2. Scroll down the page and click on **ONLINE LOGO MAKER**, as shown in the following screenshot:

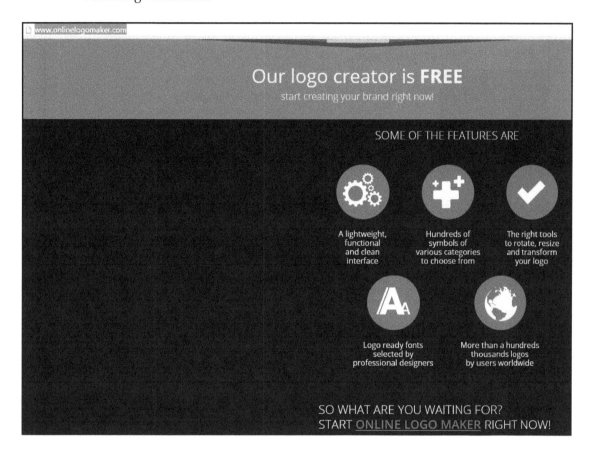

3. A new tab appears, displaying an online editor, as shown in the following screenshot:

4. Click on both the image and the text of online logo maker and click on **DELETE**. We need to delete the logo to start making our own.
5. Click on **ADD TEXT** in the left-hand margin.
6. A block with text options appears.

7. Choose the font, the color, and bold or italics before starting to write, as shown in the following screenshot:

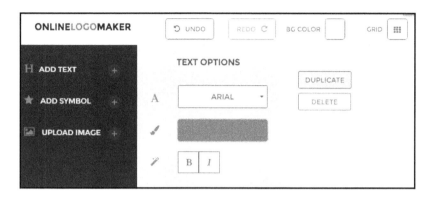

8. Click on the **Enter a text** box and write the text, as shown in the following screenshot:

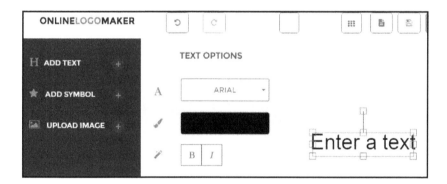

9. Write the text of the logo.
10. Click on **ADD SYMBOL**. A block appears; choose the desired category.
11. After choosing the category, images appear. Click on the desired image.
12. Choose more images if desired, and repeat the process.
13. More text can be added if desired.

14. When the logo is ready, click on **SAVE** at the top of the right-hand margin, as shown in the following screenshot:

15. A pop-up window appears, giving the information shown in the following screenshot:

16. Click on **PNG (FREE)**.
17. Click on the logo that we have just downloaded. Open it with a PNG editor, such as Paint for Windows users or Preview for iOSx users.
18. Save the file.

We have just created our logo. It's time to upload it to MoodleCloud or Moodle on-premises.

Adding the logo to MoodleCloud in the More theme

Once the logo has been created, we can replace the Moodle logo with our own. Every organization has a logo that represents it, as Moodle has its own, which is shown in the Moodle course. We have already created a logo or copied the logo of the organization that we belong to from their website.

Now, there are some steps that we need to follow in order to upload the logo to MoodleCloud. A key factor that we need to take into account is that the logo should be in .png format. These are the steps to follow:

1. Log in to MoodleCloud.
2. Click on **Site administration| Appearance | Themes | More** (in this case, it is the theme for MoodleCloud).
3. Scroll down the site and a logo block appears.
4. The maximum size of the file is 167.2 MB, so we check the size before uploading it to MoodleCloud. We can also check the pixels to customize the logo before uploading it. This is shown in the following screenshot:

1. Click on the file and both the pixels and the size are shown underneath the file.
2. If the file size is correct, we need to customize the CSS block.

3. Click on **Add**, or drag and drop the file, to upload the logo, as shown in the following screenshot:

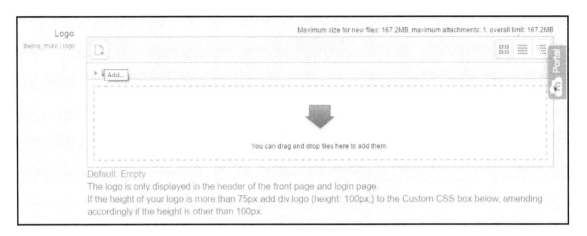

5. Highlight `div.logo {height: 100px;}`, and click on **Copy**, as shown in the following screenshot:

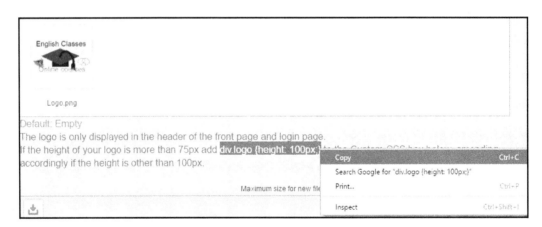

6. Paste it into the **Custom CSS** block, as shown in the following screenshot:

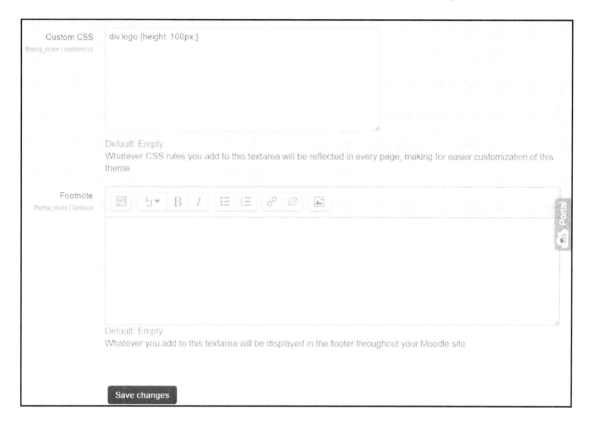

7. Click on **Save changes**. The logo is displayed in the header of the front page and the login page.

8. The logo is displayed in the header of the front page, as shown in the following screenshot:

9. The logo is displayed on the login page, as shown in the following screenshot:

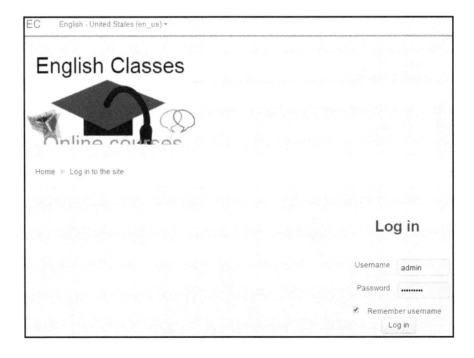

MoodleCloud is free and has some limitations; displaying the logo is one of them. If we need to customize more themes in MoodleCloud, there are more paid services; otherwise, the logo is just displayed in the header of the front page and the login page.

Another important aspect to take into account is that according to the theme that we are working with, it is the type of customization that we can do. Thus it is relevant to know which theme to use according to what we want to do.

Adding the logo to the Essential theme in Moodle on-premises

We have downloaded and installed the Essential theme in our Moodle on-premises in previous chapters, therefore we are going to add a logo to it. In order to add the logo, the steps are similar to the ones that we have followed for uploading a logo to the More theme in MoodleCloud. Therefore, we enter our Moodle on-premises course and follow these steps in order to upload the logo. We are going to use the same logo that we have created at the beginning of the chapter:

1. Enter the Moodle course.
2. Under **Administration**, click on **Site administration | Appearance | Themes | Essential | Header,** as shown in the following screenshot:

3. Scroll down the page and look for the logo block.
4. Remember to check the logo size and pixels before uploading the logo. Click on **Add** or drag and drop the file.

5. Below the **Logo** block, there are two blocks, **Logo width**, and **Logo height**, as shown in the following screenshot:

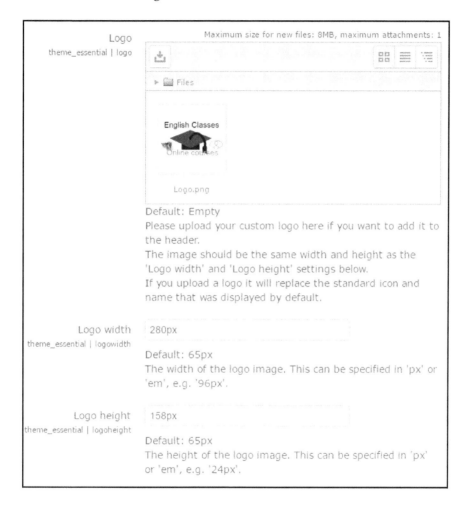

6. Scroll down the page and click on **Save changes**.

7. The logo is displayed in the header through the Moodle course. The screenshot shows the logo in the dashboard:

The following screenshot shows the logo in Site home:

Downloading a Favicon

Favicon is short for a favorite icon. It is the shortcut icon which is found in the tab. It is a file containing a small icon; we can replace the Moodle Favicon for one related to our Moodle course. The Moodle Favicon is shown in the following screenshot:

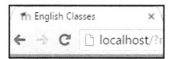

In order to change the Favicon, we need to choose a new one. There are some websites that provide us with free icons. In this example, we will use the following website: `http://www.iconarchive.com/` or `https://icons8.com/`.

Choose any icon from these websites or from any other website; there are plenty of websites which supply Favicons, so you can search for them. When a Favicon has been selected, we are ready to change it in our Moodle on-premises. In this example, we are going to work with the following Favicon:

An important thing to bear in mind is that we need to download the .ico file so that we can use it; other file extensions won't work. So, once we have selected the icon, click on it and download it as a .ico file in order to use it afterwards, and upload it to the Moodle course, as shown in the following screenshot:

Changing the Favicon in the Essential theme in Moodle on-premises

We enter our Moodle on-premises course in order to change the Favicon. We want to change the icon in order to change the profile of our course; in this way, we get rid of the Moodle icons to customize it with icon of our choosing.

To change the Favicon, we have to follow these steps:

1. Enter the Moodle course.
2. Under **Administration**, click on **Site administration** | **Appearance** | **Themes** | **Essential** | **General**.
3. Scroll down the page and find the **Custom favicon** block.
4. Click on **Add** or drag and drop the file, as shown in the following screenshot:

5. Click on **Save changes**.
6. The Favicon looks as shown in the following screenshot:

Adding a header background image in the Essential theme to Moodle on-premises

We can enhance the header of the Moodle on-premises course by adding a background image so that the logo does not appear on its own. If the organization that we are working with has a special logo with a background image, we can use it; in some cases, schools are divided into houses or categories, and each of them has a specific color. Those colors may be a part of a background image or a flag.

There are also plenty of background images that we can download, or we can create one ourselves. In this case, we are going to use an already created background image, the background of the header. These are the steps that we have to follow:

1. Under **Administration**, click on **Site administration | Appearance | Themes | Essential | Header**.
2. Scroll down until you find the **Header background image** block.
3. Click on Add or drag and drop the file of the background image to upload it.
4. Click on the down arrow next to the **Header background style** block and choose **Tiled**, as shown in the following screenshot:

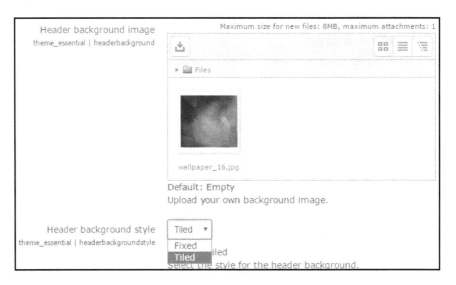

5. Scroll down and click on **Save changes**.

6. The header background image looks as shown in the following screenshot:

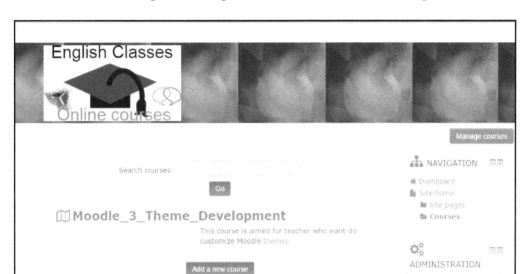

Test your knowledge

A. We can see the logo in the More MoodleCloud theme ...

 1. ...in the header of the front page and on the login page.
 2. ...in the header of the front page only.
 3. ...on the login page only.

B. If we add a logo to the Essential theme ...

 1. ...we can see the logo in the header of the front page only.
 2. ...we can see the logo in the header of all pages in the course.
 3. ...we can see the logo on the login page only.

C. Favicon is short for ...

 1. ...favorite icon.
 2. ...fabulous icon.
 3. ...neither, it's just a word for the icon in the website tab.

D. When we add a Favicon …

    1. …we have to download a `.png` file.

    2. …we have to download a `.ico` file.

    3. …we have to download a `.jpg` file.

E. Header background images can be set as tiled style …

    1. …to cover all the header below the logo.

    2. …to cover the logo, so that we cannot see it.

    3. …to appear as a simple image below the logo.

Summary

In this chapter, we have been working with UI-based settings to tune our Moodle themes. We did not have to make changes to specific files, such as HTML files or CSS, because we took advantages of a theme where we could upload a logo, Favicon, and background image as a tiled style. We have made all these changes in Moodle on-premises.

With regards to MoodleCloud, we have uploaded a logo that can then be seen in the header of the front page and the header of the login page, which is allowed in the theme that we are working with, although MoodleCloud has some limitations.

Now we are ready to make many more changes to the look and feel of Moodle on-premises and MoodleCloud in Chapter 4, *Customizing the Header and the Footer*.

4
Customizing the Header and the Footer

In this chapter, we will customize the header and the footer by adding information to our Moodle on-premises or MoodleCloud. We can easily add links or another type of information to the top and the bottom, using the header and the footer of our Moodle course. Therefore, we will work on both of them since there are some slight differences, especially since MoodleCloud has some limitations. Therefore, we will learn how to do it in both of them.

In Moodle on-premises, we will work with the Essential theme, which is complete and lets us work with plenty of customizations. Furthermore, the Essential theme is also available through most Moodle hosting companies. We will work with online HTML editors to test the customization before adding them to the Moodle course.

We will make hyperlinks to social networks in the header of Moodle on-premises, so that Moodle can communicate or look for more information. We can also create a profile on these networks to suit the Moodle course that we are working with.

We will also customize the footer of the Moodle course. We can add text or images. If we add images, we can use HTML code to avoid uploading the image to the course, as the HTML editor of the footer does not allow us to upload an image. Another option is to upload an image using Wikimedia, so we just search for an image from the file picker and click on it.

We can create a slideshow in the page area content, because we might show how the school or the university for instance work or the services offered, adding information about the course or creating some ads, as desired. The look and feel of the course will be more attractive and the more images we add, the more appealing it will be.

In this chapter, we shall cover the following topics:

- Adding footnotes in MoodleCloud
- Adding social networks to the header in the Moodle on-premises Essential theme
- Customizing the footer in the Moodle on-premises Essential theme
- Editing the front page area content
- Creating a slide show in the front page area content

Adding footnotes in MoodleCloud

We will customize the footer in MoodleCloud; we can add both text and an image using the HTML editor. We can also embed them using some code if desired. So, according to the profile of the Moodle course, we will add a footnote. It will appear throughout the course. It is different from a logo, which appears on two pages only.

In order to add a footnote, these are the steps that we have to follow:

1. Enter the Moodle course in **MoodleCloud**.
2. Click on **Appearance | Themes | MoodleCloud** (which is the theme to customize).
3. Scroll down the page and fill in the **Footnote** block, as shown in the following screenshot:

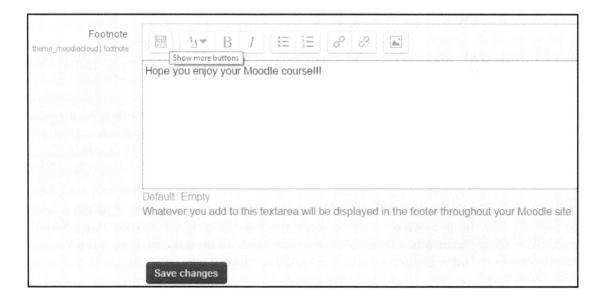

4. Click on the show more buttons icon to customize the HTML code. The following HTML editor appears:

5. Click on the **HTML** icon to customize the style of the letters.
6. Open a new tab and go to the following website: http://www.w3schools.com/html/default.asp. There is a guide on working with HTML code; try it online before working in the editor.
7. In the left-hand margin, click on **HTML Styles**, as shown in the following screenshot:

8. Scroll down the page until you see **HTML Text color**. Click on **Try it yourself**.

9. The following online editor appears:

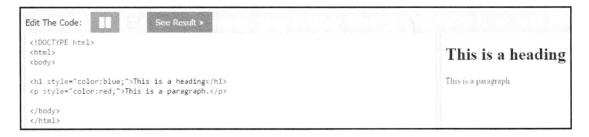

10. The code reads as follows:

```
<!DOCTYPE html>
<html>
  <body>
    <h1 style="color:blue;">This is a heading</h1>
    <p style="color:red;">This is a paragraph.</p>
  </body>
</html>
```

Highlight `This is a heading` and `This is a paragraph`. Replace them with the words that you want to add, as shown here:

```
<!DOCTYPE html>
<html>
<body>
<h1 style="color:blue;">Enjoy your course!!! </h1>
<p style="color:red;">Keep Moodling!!!.</p>
</body>
</html>
```

11. Click on **See Result**, as shown in the following screenshot:

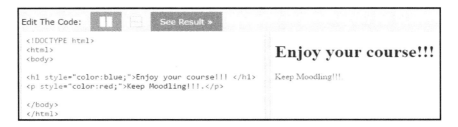

12. Copy the code.
13. Go back to **MoodleCloud** and paste it into the HTML editor in **MoodleCloud**.
14. Click on **Save changes**.
15. The footnote is shown in the following screenshot:

Adding social networks to header

We can add social network icons to the header of Moodle on-premises. Social networking is a must nowadays and there are interactions every second using these networks, so we cannot make a Moodle course without them. We must bear in mind the age of the users of the Moodle course since they may or may not be allowed to use these networks, especially if the organization is a primary or secondary school.

If the Moodle course is targeted at people who are allowed to visit social networking sites it is not a problem whatsoever, since most people have a large number of them.

We will add the icons for social networks to the header of the Essential theme. This can be done in a very simple way. Follow these steps to add social network icons:

1. Under **Administration**, click on **Site administration** | **Appearance** | **Themes** | **Essential** | **Header**.

2. Scroll down the page until you get to **Engage your users with social networking**, as shown in the following screenshot:

Engage your users with social networking

Provide direct links to the core social networks that promote your brand. These will appear in the header of every page.

Website URL
theme_essential | website

Default: Empty
Enter the URL of your own website. (i.e
http://about.me/gjbarnard)

Facebook URL
theme_essential | facebook

Default: Empty
Enter the URL of your Facebook page. (i.e
https://www.facebook.com/mycollege)

Flickr URL
theme_essential | flickr

Default: Empty
Enter the URL of your Flickr page. (i.e
http://www.flickr.com/photos/mycollege)

Twitter URL
theme_essential | twitter

Default: Empty
Enter the URL of your Twitter feed. (i.e
https://www.twitter.com/mycollege)

Google+ URL
theme_essential | googleplus

Default: Empty
Enter the URL of your Google+ profile. (i.e
https://plus.google.com/+mycollege)

LinkedIn URL

---

3. Complete the **Website URL** block; if you do not have a website, you can make free websites using `http://www.webs.com/`.

4. Complete the **Facebook URL** block; we can use a Facebook page or a profile page. Create a Facebook profile at `https://www.facebook.com/`.

5. Complete the **Flickr URL** block, or create an account at `https://www.flickr.com/`.

6. Complete the **Twitter URL** block, or create an account at `https://twitter.com/`.

7. Complete the **Google + URL** block, or create an account at `https://plus.google.com/`.

8. Complete the **LinkedIn URL** block, or create an account at `https://www.linkedin.com/`.

9. Complete the **Pinterest URL** block, or create an account at `https://www.pinterest.com/`.

10. Complete the **Instagram URL** block, or create an account by downloading the app from Google Play or iTunes.

11. Complete the **YouTube URL** block, or create an account at `https://www.youtube.com/`.

12. Complete the **Skype Account URL** block, or create an account at `https://login.skype.com/registration`.

13. Complete the **VKontake URL** block, or create an account at `http://vk.com/login`.

14. The blocks look as shown in the following screenshot:

Facebook URL theme_essential | facebook	https://www.facebook.com/silvina.hillar Default: Empty Enter the URL of your Facebook page. (i.e https://www.facebook.com/mycollege)
Flickr URL theme_essential | flickr	https://www.flickr.com/photos/silvinahillar/ Default: Empty Enter the URL of your Flickr page. (i.e http://www.flickr.com/photos/mycollege)
Twitter URL theme_essential | twitter	https://mobile.twitter.com/SilvinaHillar Default: Empty Enter the URL of your Twitter feed. (i.e https://www.twitter.com/mycollege)
Google+ URL theme_essential | googleplus	https://plus.google.com/u/0/1093206380314 Default: Empty Enter the URL of your Google+ profile. (i.e https://plus.google.com/+mycollege)
LinkedIn URL theme_essential | linkedin	https://www.linkedin.com/in/silvina-hillar-382 Default: Empty Enter the URL of your LinkedIn profile. (i.e https://www.linkedin.com/company/mycollege)
Pinterest URL theme_essential | pinterest	https://www.pinterest.com/silvinahillar/ Default: Empty Enter the URL of your Pinterest page. (i.e http://pinterest.com/mycollege/mypinboard)
Instagram URL theme_essential | instagram	https://www.instagram.com/silvina.hillar/

15. If some social networks are not necessary, feel free to choose only the ones you want to add. In this example, all the blocks were filled in, except for Skype.

16. Scroll down the page and click on **Save changes**.

17. The header looks as shown in the following screenshot:

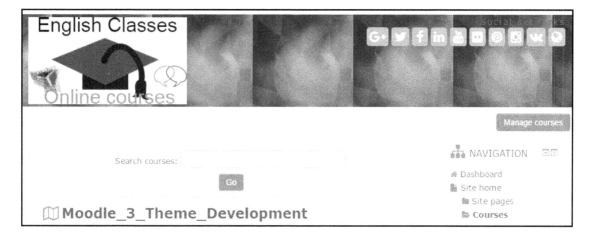

18. When hovering the mouse over the icons of the social networks, they change color, that is to say, it has got the colors that we know of, as shown in the following screenshot:

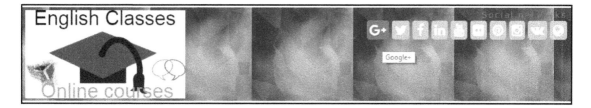

Customizing the footer in Moodle on-premises Essential theme

We can add a footnote to the footer in Moodle on-premises. Whatever we write as a footnote appears throughout the Moodle course, so we need to choose a message or a slogan that represents the profile of the Moodle site. In this example, we are going to add a message, as we have already done in MoodleCloud. So we enter Moodle on-premises and follow these steps:

1. Under **Administration**, click on **Site administration** | **Appearance** | **Themes** | **Essential** | **Footer**.
2. Complete the Copyright block by writing the name of the organization.
3. Add an image in the Footer block. Go to the following website: `https://icons8.com/web-app/for/ios7/school`.
4. Click on the desired icon, as shown in the following screenshot:

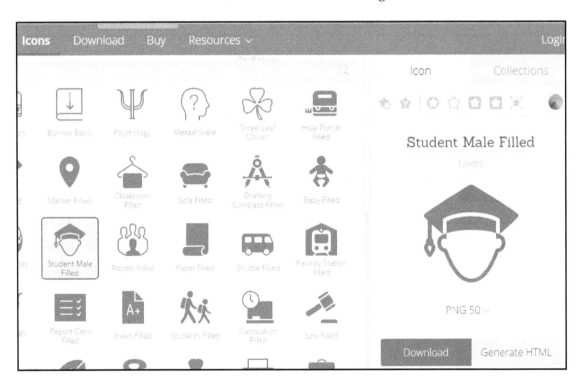

5. The selected icon appears in the right-hand margin, as shown in the previous screenshot.

6. A menu appears on the icon. The icon can be customized if desired.

7. After customizing the icon, click on **Generate HTML**. A window pops up, showing the code.

8. Highlight the code and copy it, as shown in the following screenshot:

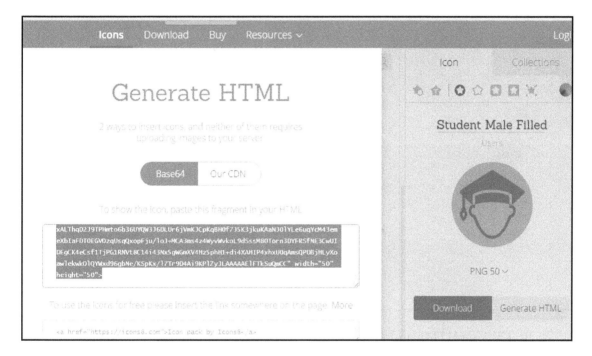

9. Go back to the Moodle on-premises course and click on the Show more buttons icon, as shown in the following screenshot:

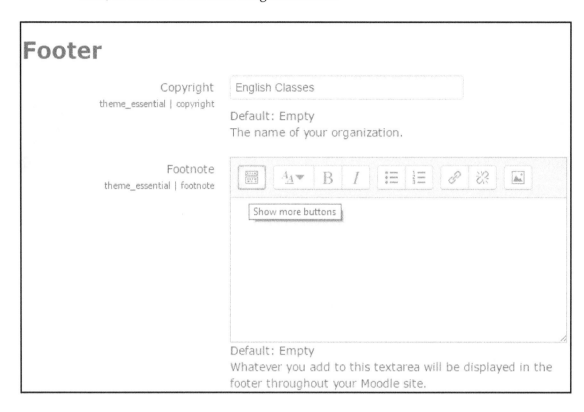

10. Click on **HTML** and paste the code that we have copied from the image.
11. Click on **HTML** again and the image appears in the HTML editor.
12. Scroll down the page and click on **Save changes**.
13. The footer looks as shown in the following screenshot:

Editing front page area content

We can edit the front page area content using four blocks. The blocks that we will edit are the ones located under the heading. We can add any valuable information or images to enhance the look and feel of the Moodle course. In this case, we will also customize the Essential theme for Moodle on-premises. The blocks that we will work with are **FRONT PAGE AREA CONTENT**, **MARKETING SPOT ONE**, **MARKETING SPOT 2**, and **MARKETING SPOT 3**. They are shown in the following screenshot:

The screenshot shows the location of the blocks to edit. The location described in the section that we will work with is the full width of the page between the slide show and the Marketing spots. The following steps are a guide to how to customize and edit these blocks using information related to the Moodle course. These are the steps that we have to follow:

1. Under **Administration**, click on **Site administration** | **Appearance** | **Themes** | **Essential** | **Front page**.
2. Scroll down the page and complete the **Front page content area contents** block, as shown in the following screenshot:

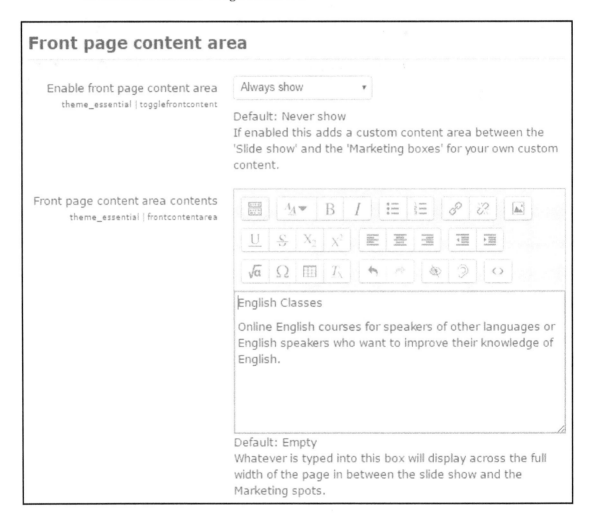

3. Scroll down the page until the **Marketing spot one** block.
4. Complete the **Title** block.
5. Click on Add icon in the **Image** block.
6. Click on **Wikimedia** and complete the **Search for** block, as shown in the following screenshot:

7. Click on **Submit**.
8. Click on the desired image.

9. Click on **Select this file**. The blocks look as shown in the following screenshot:

Marketing spot one

Enter the settings for your marketing spot.

Title	Online English courses
theme_essential | marketing1	
	Default: Empty
	Title to show in this marketing spot

Icon	
theme_essential | marketing1icon	
	Default: star
	Name of the icon you wish to use. List is here. Just enter what is after "fa-", e.g. "star".

Image	Maximum size for new files: 8MB, maximum attachments: 1
theme_essential | marketing1image	

▶ 📁 Files

Elearning6.png

Default: Empty
This provides the option of displaying an image above the text in the marketing spot

10. Repeat steps 3 to 9 for the **Marketing spot two** and **Marketing spot three** blocks.
11. Scroll down the page and click on **Save changes**.
12. Click on **Site home**.

13. The changes are shown in the following screenshot:

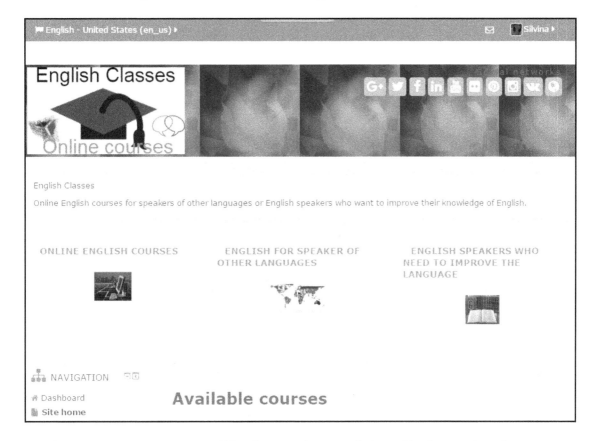

The front page customization will be shown when we click on **Site home**; the other pages will not show this customization, which we have to bear in mind.

Creating a slide show in the front page area content

We can create a slide show in the front page area content. We can design the slides in the Moodle course. We will continue customizing the Essential theme in Moodle on-premises. The slides form a dynamic slide show of up to sixteen slides in order to promote important elements of the site. They can also add more information about the services offered as well as the courses depending on whom the Moodle course is for.

In the example, we will create four slides. If no image is selected, the Moodle icon is to be shown, therefore it is recommended to add an image together with captions.

In order to create a slide show, these are the steps that we have to follow:

1. Under **Administration**, click on **Site administration | Appearance | Themes | Essential | Slide show**.
2. Click on the down arrow next to the **Number of slides** block and choose **4** (the maximum number is 16), as shown in the following screenshot:

Slide show

Dynamic slide show for the front page

This creates a dynamic slide show of up to sixteen slides for you to promote important elements of your site. The show is responsive where image height is set according to screen size. The recommended height is 300px. The width is set at 100% and therefore the actual height will be smaller if the width is greater than the screen size. At smaller screen sizes the height is reduced dynamically without the need to provide separate images. For reference screen width < 767px = height 165px, width between 768px and 979px = height 225px and width > 980px = height 300px. If no image is selected for a slide, then the default_slide image in the pix folder is used.

Toggle slide show display
theme_essential | toggleslideshow

Always show

Default: Always show
Choose if you wish to hide or show the slide show.

Number of slides
theme_essential | numberofslides

4

Default: 4
Number of slides on the slider.

3. Scroll down the page and choose the **Slide caption text color**.
4. Choose the **Slide caption background color**.

5. Click on the desired **Slide caption options**, as shown in the following screenshot:

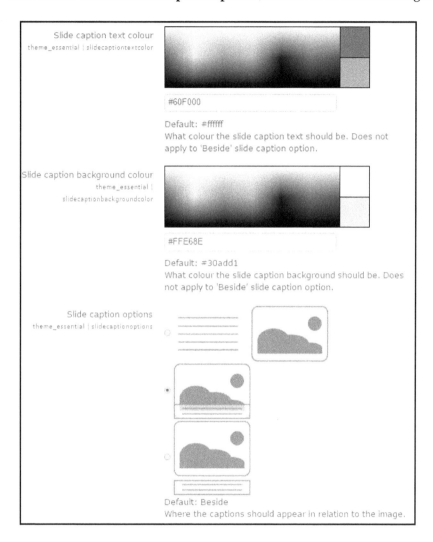

6. When scrolling down, there are plenty of options to customize the color of slides, so choose the desired colors.
7. Scroll down the page until **Slide 1**. Complete the **Slide title** block.
8. Complete the **Slide image** block.

9. Complete the **Slide caption** block, as shown in the following screenshot:

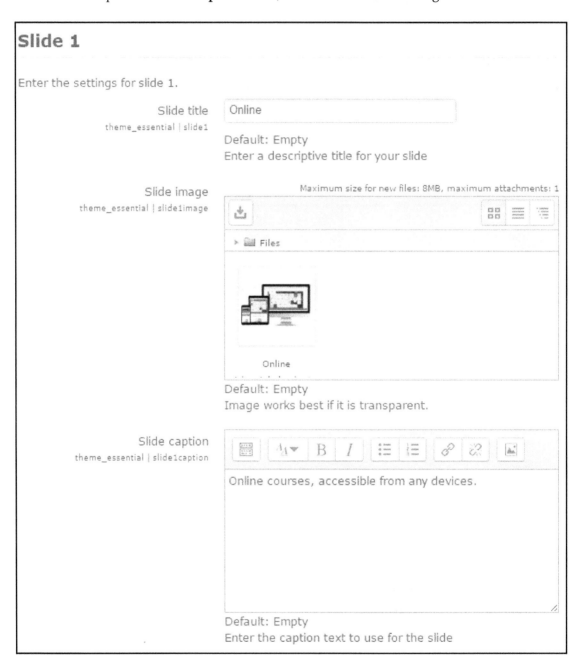

10. Repeat steps 7 to 9 and completes the slide 2, 3, and 4 blocks.
11. Click on **Save changes**.
12. Click on **Site home** to see the slide show. The slide show looks as shown in the following screenshots:

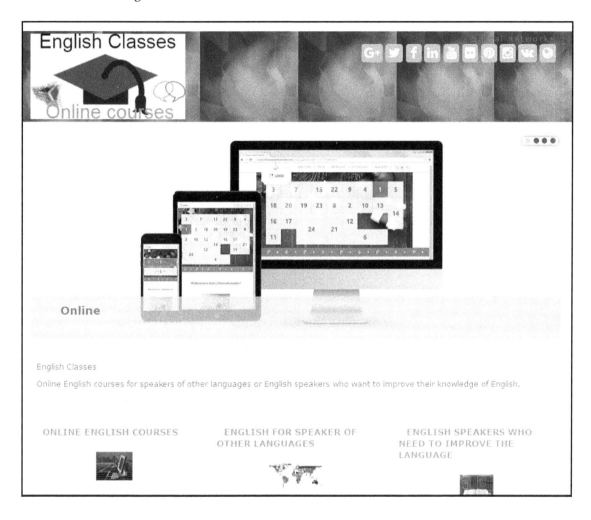

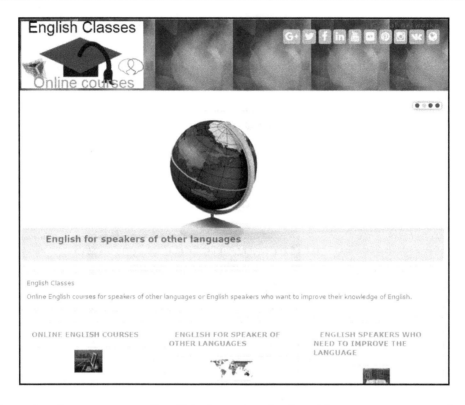

When hovering the mouse over the slide show, two horizontal arrows appear, as shown in the following screenshot from slide 3:

The last slide is shown in the following screenshot:

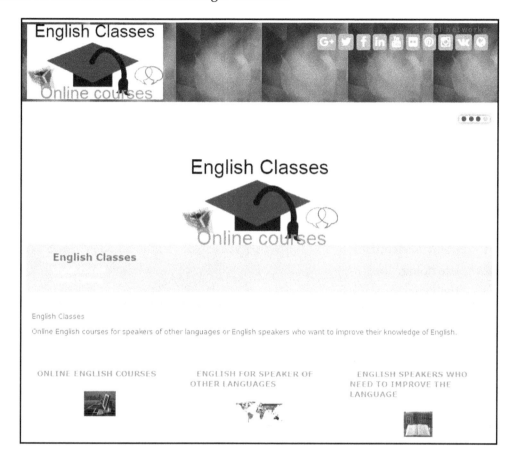

The slides are shown on the front page; they are not displayed on other pages of the course.

Test your knowledge

A. If we customize the footnote in MoodleCloud …

> 1. …we can see it throughout the course.
>
> 2. …we can see it in the header of the front page only.
>
> 3. …we can see it on the login page only.

B. We can add links to social networks in the Essential theme in Moodle on-premises by …

1. …editing HTML code.
2. …adding the URL to the belonging blocks under Header within **Theme |
   Appearance**.
3. …editing widgets from websites and pasting the HTML code.

C. If we want to add an image to the footer …

1. …we can do it using HTML code.
2. …we can upload an image to the course and use it as the footer.
3. …we can't do it.

D. When we customize the front page area we can see it in …

1. …the whole course.
2. …site home.
3. …the login page.

E. We can add …

1. …not more than 16 slides.
2. …however many slides we want.
3. …four slides, as shown in the example.

Summary

In this chapter, we have learned how to add images and text to the footer and the header. We have also added hyperlinks to social networks in Moodle on-premises. As well as that, we have also added a slide show and modified the front page, changing the look and feel of the Moodle course. We have made some changes to MoodleCloud, taking into account its limitations. There are customizable areas, though.

We are ready to keep on changing the look and feel of Moodle on-premises and MoodleCloud in the next chapter, in which we will customize elements with CSS.

5
Customizing Elements with CSS

In this chapter, we will change the look and feel of our Moodle course, focusing on sizing images and changing colors and fonts, among other things. We will be customizing the elements with **Cascading Style Sheets** (**CSS**).

In order to work with CSS, we will work with both online and offline text editors before making the changes in Moodle on-premise, so as to check how the element changes before making it definite. In this chapter, we will further our knowledge in CSS a little more and learn what we can do with it in order to change the look and feel of Moodle on-premises.

CSS is used to apply styles to the elements in order to change certain attributes of those elements. In this way, we can improve the look and feel in order to make it more attractive.

Text editors are a great tool to bear in mind when changing the look and feel of the Moodle course, since we are making the changes, and at the same time, checking how they look before working with the code in Moodle. Therefore, after checking how it looks and whether it works, we can paste the code in Moodle on-premises. Moreover, we are testing and avoiding making mistakes.

In this chapter, we will learn the following topics:

- Customizing the height and width of an element with CSS
- Setting the height and width of an image element with CSS
- Locating the information of an image element
- Customizing the height and width of an element in Moodle on-premises with CSS
- Customizing the height and width of an element in MoodleCloud with CSS
- Using the Sublime Text editor to edit code
- Locating the information of a title element
- Customizing styles of elements using the enjoycss website
- Editing the code to customize the style of elements
- Testing the code
- Changing the elements in Moodle on-premises

Customizing the height and width of an element with CSS

In previous chapters, we have learned how to add a logo to our Moodle course. In this chapter, we will learn how to customize the logo and how to change the number of pixels so that it fits the right height, by customizing our CSS.

Furthermore, we will use an online editor to understand how CSS works with an image and how the number of pixels varies. We can control the height and width of an element using CSS dimension properties. The height and width are automatically set to auto, that is to say, it is calculated by default by the browser.

In this case, we will change the default dimensions of the element. Therefore, these are the steps that we need to follow:

1. Enter http://www.w3schools.com/css/default.asp.
2. In the left-hand margin, click on **CSS Height/Width**, as shown in the following screenshot:

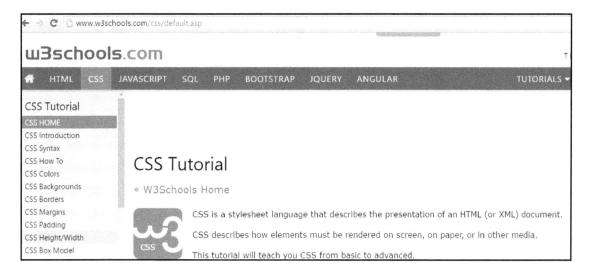

3. Read the information provided about height and width. Click on **Try it Yourself**, as shown in the following screenshot:

4. A new tab appears showing the code on the left-hand margin and the element on the right-hand margin. It is shown in the following screenshot:

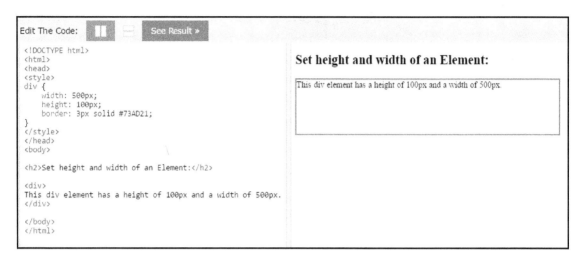

5. The code reads as follows:

```
<!DOCTYPE html>
<html>
<head>
<style>
div {
     width: 500px;
     height: 100px;
     border: 3px solid #73AD21;
}
</style>
</head>
<body>
<h2>Set height and width of an Element:</h2>
<div>
This div element has a height of 100px and a width of 500px.
</div>
</body>
</html>
```

6. Width and height are measured in **pixels** (**px**); therefore, if we edit the code, we can change the size of the information box.

7. Change the code as follows:

```
div {
    width: 400px;
    height: 80px;
    border: 3px solid #73AD21;
}
```

8. Change the code for the data inside the information box, as follows:

```
<div>
This div element has a height of 80px and a width of 400px.
</div>
```

9. Click on **See Result**.

10. The result is shown on the right-hand side. The information box is smaller and the information has changed. It is shown in the following screenshot:

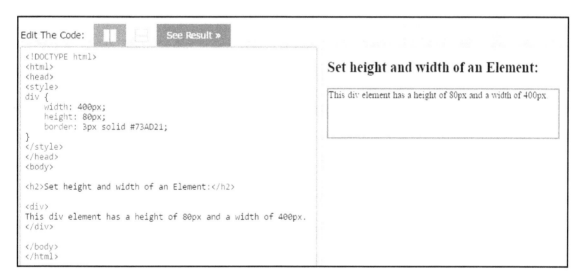

In the previous example, we did not need to code from scratch, we just located the code that we needed to change. We will work on another example before working with CSS on the Moodle course. In the following example, we will change the height and width of an image.

Setting the height and width of an image element with CSS

We can change the height and width of elements such as images. In this example, we will continue using the editor and we will work with an example of an image to learn how to locate it within the code. Thus, we need to visit the following website: http://www.w3schoo ls.com/css/css_dimension.asp (the website from the previous example).

Follow these steps to set the height and width of an image element:

1. Scroll down until you find **Try it Yourself – Examples**, as shown in the following screenshot:

 Try it Yourself - Examples

Set the height and width of elements
This example demonstrates how to set the height and width of different elements.

2. Click on **Set the height and width of Elements**, as shown in the previous screenshot.

3. A new tab appears displaying code on the left-hand side and the elements on the right-hand side, that is to say, images and information. It looks as shown in the following screenshot:

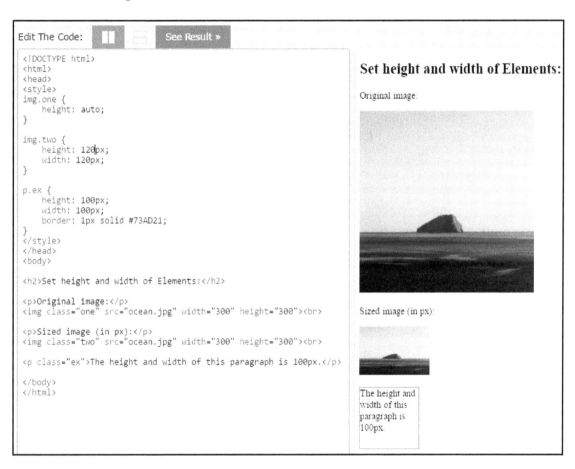

4. The code reads as follows:

```
<!DOCTYPE html>
<html>
<head>
<style>
img.one {
    height: auto;
}
img.two {
    height: 120px;
    width: 120px;
}
p.ex {
    height: 100px;
    width: 100px;
    border: 1px solid #73AD21;
}
</style>
</head>
<body>
<h2>Set height and width of Elements:</h2>
<p>Original image:</p>
<img class="one" src="ocean.jpg" width="300" height="300"><br>
<p>Sized image (in px):</p>
<img class="two" src="ocean.jpg" width="300" height="300"><br>
<p class="ex">
  The height and width of this paragraph is 100px.</p>
</body>
</html>
```

5. The size of the first element (image) is automatic, therefore we won't change it. The size of the second element (image) is 120px both for height and width. It is shown in the following code:

```
img.two {
    height: 120px;
    width: 120px;
}
```

6. Change the number of pixels for the second element (image). Change from `120px` (120 pixels) to `80px` for both height and width. It is shown in the following code:

```
img.two {
    height: 80px;
    width: 80px;
}
```

7. Click on **See Result**.

8. The new element size is shown in the following screenshot:

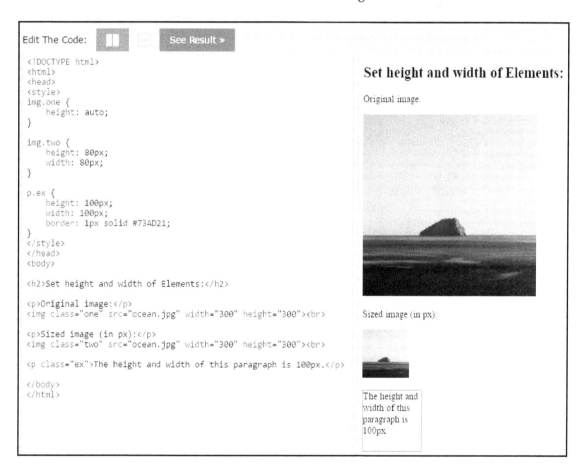

9. Compare the size of the element. On the left is **120px for height and width**, and on the right is **80px for height and width**, as shown in the following screenshot:

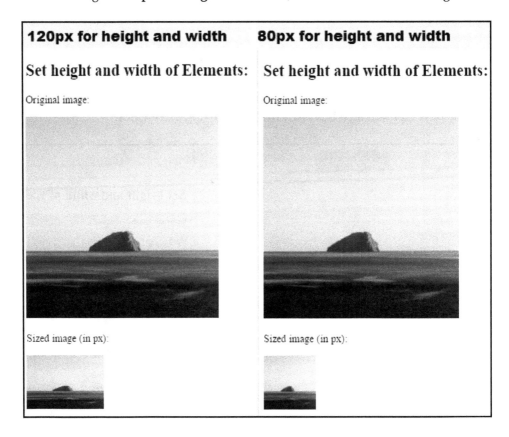

Locating the information of an image element

Before customizing the height and width of an element in Moodle on-premises with CSS, we need to locate the information of said element. It is not a very difficult task because we have already been working with similar information. Therefore, we need to enter Moodle on-premises's site and proceed with the following steps:

1. Right-click on the logo and click on **Inspect**, as shown in the following screenshot:

2. Information about the element appears, as shown in the following screenshot:

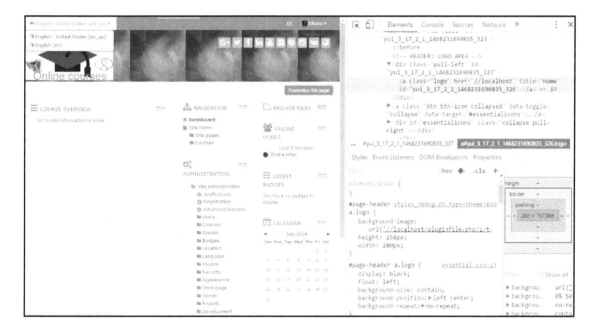

3. The following code appears, highlighted in the previous screenshot; it reads as follows:

```
<a class="logo" href="//localhost"
    id="yui_3_17_2_1_1468231690835_326"></a>
```

4. The following code defines the element and its style:

```
#page-header
a.logo
```

5. The height is 158px and its width is 200px. The information is shown highlighted in the following screenshot:

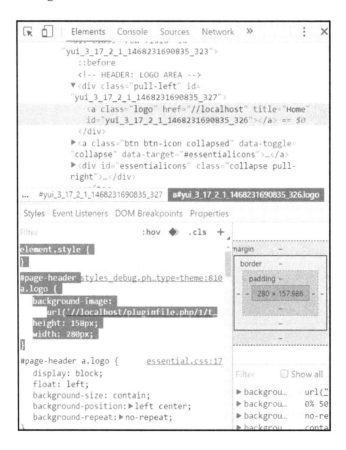

Customizing the height and width of an element in Moodle on-premises with CSS

We can customize the height and width of an element in Moodle on-premises with CSS. In this example, we will customize the height and width of the logo that we have inserted in previous chapters. As we have just learned how to find the information to be able to change with CSS, we will do it in our Moodle on-premises. These are the steps that we have to follow:

1. Within the **administration** block, click on **Site administration** | **Appearance** | **Themes** | **Essential** | **General**.
2. Scroll down until you find **Custom CSS**, as shown in the following screenshot:

3. Copy the code that gives the information of the element whose height and width are going to change. While copying the code, the element appears, as shown in the following screenshot:

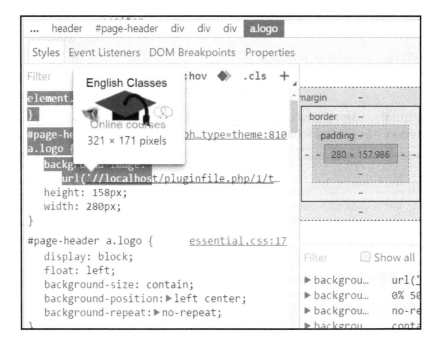

4. The code reads as follows:

```
element.style {
}
#page-header a.logo {
    background-image:
    url('//localhost/pluginfile.php/1/theme_essential
      /logo/-1/Logo.png');
    height: 158px;
    width: 280px;
}
```

5. Paste the code within the **Customs CSS** block, as shown in the following screenshot:

Custom CSS
theme_essential | customcss

```
element.style {
}
#page-header a.logo {
    background-image:
url('//localhost/pluginfile.php/1/theme_essential/logo/-1/Logo.png
');
    height: 158px;
    width: 280px;
}
```

Default: Empty
Whatever CSS rules you add to this textarea will be reflected in every page, making for easier customization of this theme.

6. Edit the height and width of the element; the code reads as follows:

```
element.style {
}
#page-header a.logo {
    background-image:
    url('//localhost/pluginfile.php/1/theme_essential
        /logo/-1/Logo.png');
height: 100px;
width: 200px;
}
```

We have made changes to the element with a class that is equal to the logo and is included within a div with an ID equal to the page header.

7. Click on **Save changes**.

8. The following screenshot shows the size of the image before editing the CSS code:

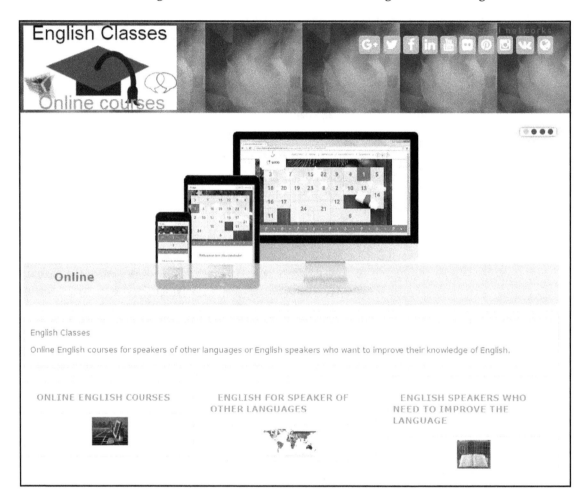

9. The following screenshot shows the size of the image after editing the CSS code:

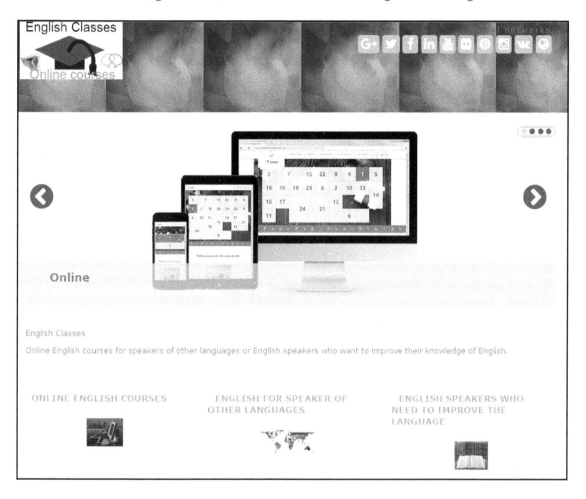

Customizing the height and width of an element in MoodleCloud with CSS

We can customize the height and width of an element in MoodleCloud with CSS. In this example, we will customize the logo that we have already inserted. As we have learned how to find the information to change withing CSS code we will do it in our MoodleCloud. After logging in MoodleCloud, these are the steps that we have to follow:

1. Under **Site administration**, click on **Appearance** | **Themes** | **Moodlecloud**.

2. Scroll down until you find **Custom CSS**, as shown in the following screenshot:

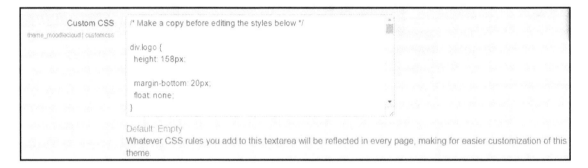

3. The code reads as follows:

```
div.logo {
   height: 158px;

   margin-bottom: 20px;
   float: none;
}
```

4. Highlight 158px and change it to 100px, as shown in the following screenshot:

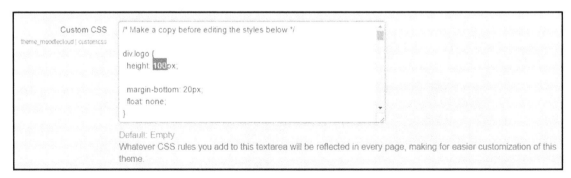

5. Scroll down and click on Save changes. The logo's size is as shown in the following screenshot:

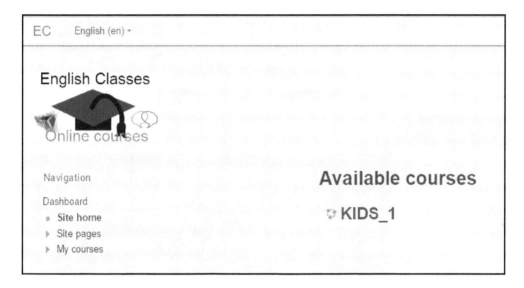

Using Sublime Text to edit code

We use Sublime Text because it is a colorized and highlighted syntax text editor and we can identify the code easily. Furthermore, Sublime Text is available for OS X, Windows, and Linux. In order to work with Sublime Text, follow these steps:

1. Visit the following website: `https://www.sublimetext.com/`.

2. Click on **Download**, as shown in the following screenshot:

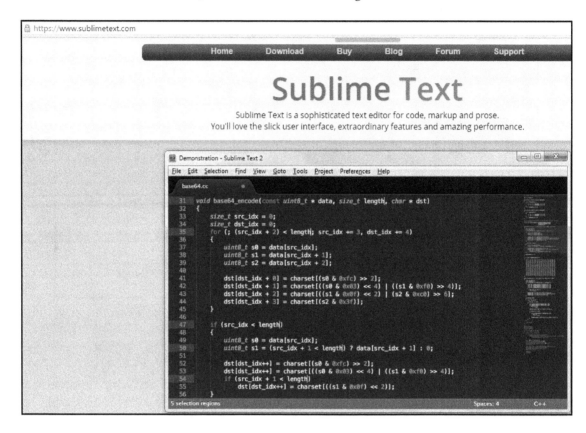

3. Download Sublime Text for free in order to evaluate it and then a license must be purchased to continue using it, as shown in the following screenshot:

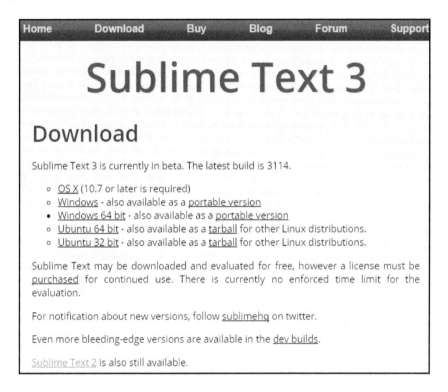

4. After installing Sublime Text, run it.
5. Copy the code that has just been edited from the Moodle course.

6. Paste it in Sublime Text, as shown in the following screenshot:

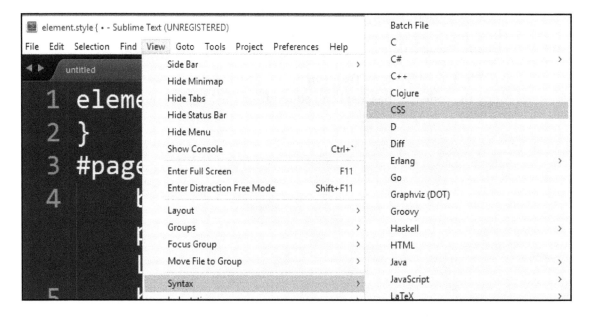

7. The text is plain without any colors whatsoever. Click on **View** | **Syntax** | **CSS**, as shown in the following screenshot:

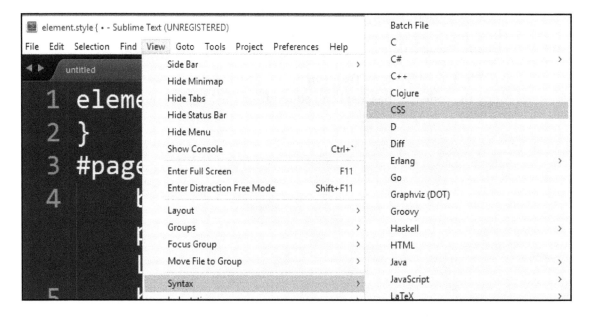

8. The code looks colorized and highlighted, as shown in the following screenshot:

```
File  Edit  Selection  Find  View  Goto  Tools  Project  Preferences  Help
  untitled              element.style |           element.style |
1 element.style {
2 }
3 #page-header a.logo {
4     background-image: url('//localhost/pluginfile.php/1/theme_essential/
5     height: 100px;
6     width: 200px;
7 }
```

Because the code is colorized and highlighted and not just plaintext, it allows us to more easily spot what we need to edit, therefore making it easier to work with.

Locating the information of a title element

We can change the styles of different elements, among other things, and as long as we learn how to edit CSS, we can completely change the look and feel of our Moodle on-premises. Step by step, we can learn how to identify the different elements so as to make changes to them.

In this example, we will locate the titles in order to add changes to them. First of all, we need to inspect the element in order to edit code and enhance it. We will change the font and size of the letters. After logging into Moodle on-premises, these are the steps that we have to follow:

1. Highlight the element to inspect and right-click on it.

2. Click on **Inspect**, as shown in the following screenshot:

3. The code appears, and you need to identify the element.

4. The element is shown highlighted in the following screenshot:

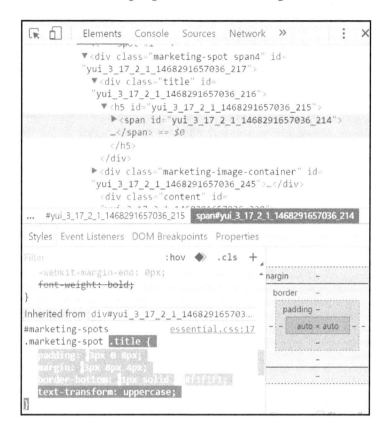

5. The code reads as follows:

```css
.title {
    padding: 3px 0 8px;
    margin: 3px 8px 4px;
    border-bottom: 1px solid #f1f1f1;
    text-transform: uppercase;
}
```

After locating the element, we need to make changes. In order to make changes to the element, we need to know how to code them using CSS. Fortunately, we can do it using an online editor through which we can edit the code shown earlier.

Customizing styles of elements using the enjoycss website

We can generate the desired changes without editing code in our Moodle on-premises first. There are code generators that save us time, so we don't need to learn how to write the code. We can generate code just by clicking on the desired changes and adding them to the theme.

Furthermore, there is an added benefit in that we are not changing our Moodle course and making mistakes when coding directly in it. This is an example to follow, but we can combine the steps in order to generate another code and in that way, we generate other changes in the look and feel of the theme.

Therefore, we can follow these steps in order to enhance the titles in the Moodle theme. These are the steps that we have to follow:

1. Enter `http://enjoycss.com/`.
2. Click on **Blank**, as shown in the following screenshot:

3. The editor appears, as shown in the following screenshot:

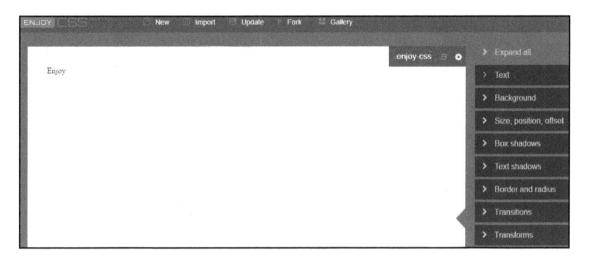

4. Click on **Text**, on the right-hand side.
5. A window displaying a menu appears. Here you can make changes to the word **Enjoy**.
6. Click on the color picker and choose the desired color.

7. Choose the font, size, and type of letter. The changes will be reflected in the word Enjoy, as shown in the following screenshot:

8. Click on the other items of the menu to add more changes to the word Enjoy, for instance, **Background**.

9. Click on **add color** and choose the desired color, as shown in the following screenshot:

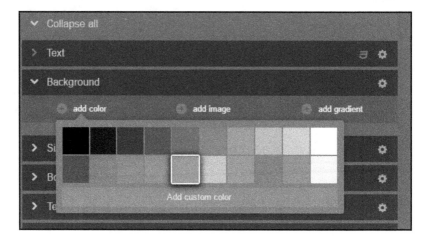

10. After getting the desired changes, click on **Get the Code**, in the lower-right corner, as shown in the following screenshot:

11. Another screen appears, displaying the code.
12. On the upper ribbon, the different web browsers, as well as mobile devices, appear. This is where the code works. Click on the downwards arrow to change the version.

13. Hover the mouse over the right-hand margin. A message appears that says **Copy to clipboard**. Click on it. It is shown in the following screenshot:

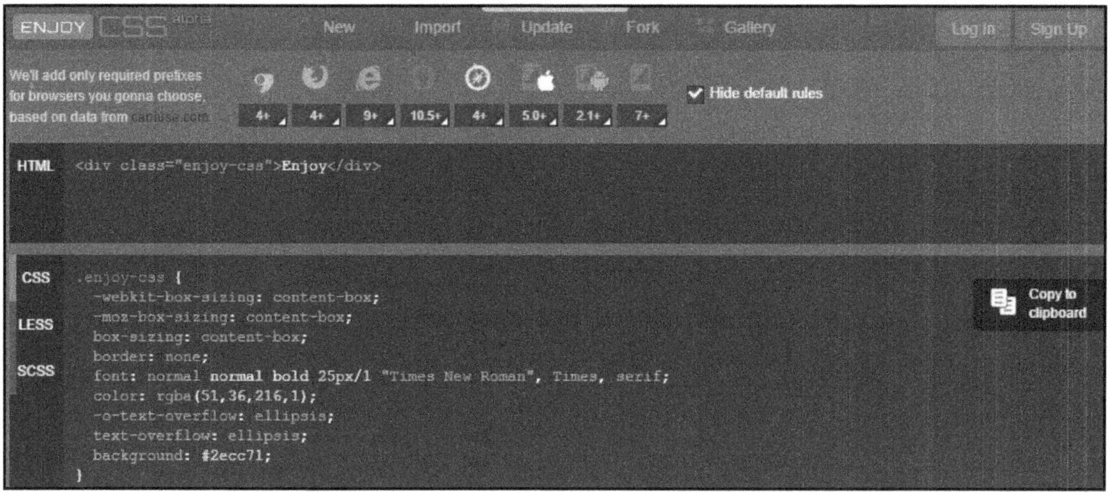

14. A message appears in a pop-up window that says **Copied**, as shown in the following screenshot:

15. The code reads as follows:

```
.enjoy-css {
  -webkit-box-sizing: content-box;
  -moz-box-sizing: content-box;
  box-sizing: content-box;
  border: none;
  font: normal normal bold 25px/1
  "Times New Roman", Times, serif;
  color: rgba(51,36,216,1);
  -o-text-overflow: ellipsis;
  text-overflow: ellipsis;
  background: #2ecc71;
}
```

Editing the code to customize the style of elements

We have just edited the code to make changes to the word **Enjoy**. However, we do not have, or can't modify, that word because the code won't work. As we want to add the changes made to it, we need to edit the codes that we have copied so far. We will work with Sublime Text in order to edit the code. Therefore, run Sublime Text and follow these steps:

1. Enter Sublime Text and paste the following code, which we have inspected and copied from our Moodle on-premises. The code reads as follows:

    ```
    .title {
        padding: 3px 0 8px;
        margin: 3px 8px 4px;
        border-bottom: 1px solid #f1f1f1;
        text-transform: uppercase;
    }
    ```

2. Copy the code that we generated in `http://enjoycss.com/code/`.

3. Paste the code in Sublime Text. It is shown in the following screenshot:

```
File  Edit  Selection  Find  View  Goto  Tools  Project  Preferences  Help

  ◄ ►   Code_05.css

 1  .title {
 2      .enjoy-css {
 3   -webkit-box-sizing: content-box;
 4   -moz-box-sizing: content-box;
 5   box-sizing: content-box;
 6   border: none;
 7   font: normal normal bold 25px/1 "Times New Roman", Times, serif;
 8   color: rgba(51,36,216,1);
 9   -o-text-overflow: ellipsis;
10   text-overflow: ellipsis;
11   background: #2ecc71;
12  }
13      padding: 3px 0 8px;
14      margin: 3px 8px 4px;
15   border-bottom: 1px solid #f1f1f1;
16   text-transform: uppercase;
17  }
```

4. Edit the code so it reads as follows:

```
.title {
  -webkit-box-sizing: content-box;
  -moz-box-sizing: content-box;
  box-sizing: content-box;
  border: none;
  font: normal normal bold 25px/1
    "Times New Roman", Times, serif;
  color: rgba(51,36,216,1);
  -o-text-overflow: ellipsis;
  text-overflow: ellipsis;
  background: #2ecc71;
    padding: 3px 0 8px;
    margin: 3px 8px 4px;
    border-bottom: 1px solid #f1f1f1;
    text-transform: uppercase;
}
```

If desired, we can paste the code in Moodle in order to change the element that we have been working with; on the other hand, it is advisable to test it before changing it, which is the next step that we will follow.

Testing the code

Before adding changes to Moodle on-premises, it is advisable to test the code. As we have already edited the code, we have to make sure that we have not made any mistakes and that it works. Therefore, we can test it using `https://jsfiddle.net/`. These are the steps that you have to follow:

1. Enter `https://jsfiddle.net/`.
2. Go back to `http://enjoycss.com/` and copy the HTML code, as shown in the following screenshot:

HTML `<div class="enjoy-css">Enjoy</div>`

3. Go back to `https://jsfiddle.net/` and paste the code in the HTML block.

4. Edit the code as follows:

   ```
   <div class="title">title</div>
   ```

5. Go back to Sublime Text and copy the code.

6. Go back to `https://jsfiddle.net/` and paste the code in the CSS block.

7. Click on **Run**, in the left-hand side margin. The changes are seen in the following screenshot. They are made to the word **TITLE**:

Changing the elements in Moodle on-premises

It is time to add the changes to Moodle on-premises. The steps that we have to follow are very simple; just copy and paste the CSS code that we have just edited. We know that it works because we have already tested it. Therefore, these are the steps that we have to follow:

1. Enter Moodle on-premises to edit the code.

2. Within the **Administration** block, click on **Site administration** | **Appearance** | **Themes** | **Essential** | **General**.

3. Scroll down until you find **Custom CSS**.

4. Do not erase the code you find written in the block unless you want to edit it. It is the code to change the size of the image.

5. Scroll down the block and paste the new code, as shown in the following screenshot:

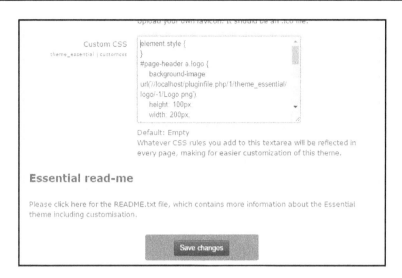

6. Click on **Save changes**. The first screenshot shows the titles before the change:

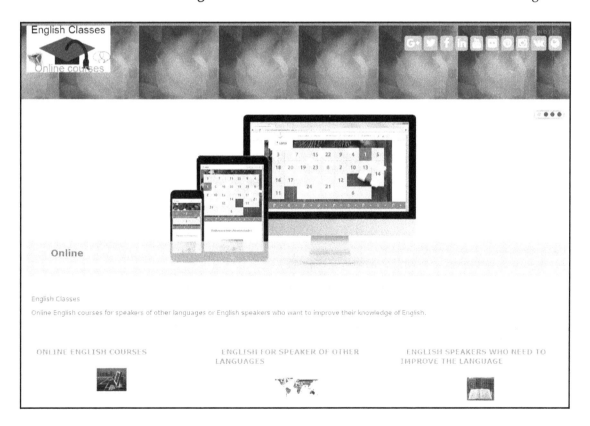

7. The following image shows the titles after editing the code:

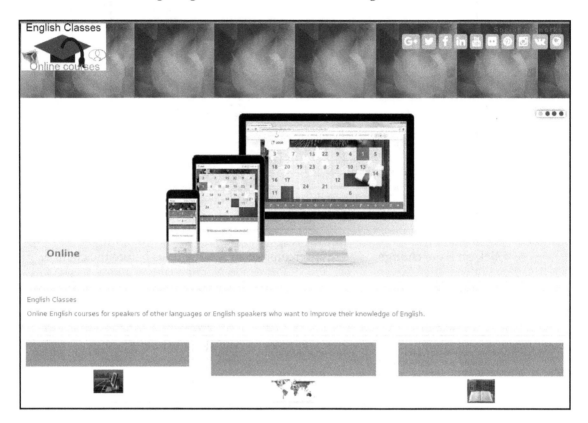

Test your knowledge

A. To customize the size of an image …

1. …we need to edit CSS code.
2. …we click on the image and resize it.
3. …we need to inspect the code, edit it, and save the changes to resize it.

B. The Essential theme lets us customize CSS …

    1. …if we download a plugin.

    2. …within the Site administration menu.

    3. …inspecting the elements.

C. Course themes …

    1. …can't be customized.

    2. …can be partially customized.

    3. …are better when not customized.

D. The Essential Moodle theme …

    1. …allows us to edit CSS.

    2. …does not allow us to edit CSS.

E. Online editors …

    1. …let us edit code and make changes in Moodle.

    2. …let us edit code and see the changes in Moodle without making them.

    3. …let us edit code and see the changes in order not to make mistakes in Moodle.

Summary

In summary, in this chapter, we have worked with several online text editors so as to learn more about CSS and what we can do in order to change the look and feel of Moodle on-premises. We have also tested the code before making any changes to avoid making mistakes. The look and feel of Moodle is completely different from the one that we had at the beginning of the book, so let's keep on making changes. In the next chapter, we will deal with icons.

6
Locating, Editing, and Using New Icons

In order to modify or completely customize the look and feel of our Moodle course, we also need to pay special attention to icons. We can edit them in order to personalize them and change the layout and see them differently.

Creating icons is more than just developing an image. Icons are saved as **Scalable Vector Graphics** (**SVG**), therefore this chapter explains how to work with different types of vector graphics formats. We will use diverse, free, and open source tools to edit, enhance, and convert the different vector graphics files.

Different types of vector graphics are involved in this chapter because they can enhance the look and feel of the Moodle course. We can not only use them but also modify them. We can change the vector graphic in order to use a part of it.

We will cover not just changing the icons (vector graphics) in our Moodle course, but also using them in other types of software in order to customize them and export them. We will be working mainly with **Inkscape** to edit the vector graphics.

Inkscape is free and open source vector drawing software that is used in order to perform certain steps. It will allow us to work with many vector assets in several file formats and export them as .png format.

We can either design the SVG (the icon) or look for one on the Internet and learn how to do it. Then, we can change it. Another possibility is to customize the existing icon and change it in our Moodle course.

Icons are a great asset to take into account since they look more appealing when they are not the ordinary ones. Furthermore, they can cope with the profile of the Moodle course.

 This chapter is focused on Moodle on-premises and some hosting services will allow the use of custom icons since MoodleCloud doesn't allow us to customize the icons.

In this chapter, we shall learn the following topics:

- Locate the icons in our Moodle on-premises course
- Locate the icon file in the server
- Download Inkscape
- Edit an SVG file
- Convert SVG files to PNG files
- Check the properties of the PNG file
- Replace the SVG file
- Replace the PNG file
- Test the new icon in Moodle on-premises
- Locate **Add an activity or resource** icons in our Moodle on-premises
- Render parts of icons
- Upload rendered icons in Moodle on-premises

Locating the icons in our Moodle on-premises course

The first step that we need to take to change the icons is to locate them. Therefore, we need to enter our Moodle on-premises course. The icons that we will change are the ones which indicate the activities or resources. We will not add an activity to the Moodle course, but we will pay attention to the icons below them. Thus, these are the steps that we have to follow:

1. Enter Moodle on-premises course and log in.
2. Click **Turn editing on**.

3. Click **Add an activity or resource**, as shown in the following screenshot:

Different icons appear next to both activities and resources. What we will change, or customize, are the icons that appear next to each activity or resource. As we have already located the icons in Moodle on-premises, we need to locate the icons in the server.

We will change the icon of the Quiz.

Locating the icon file in the server

It is time to locate the icon file in the server in order to see the type of file, as well as where to save the new icon that we want to use afterwards. In order to use a new icon, we need to replace the one that is being used.

In the previous tip, we mentioned that we would change the quiz icon file therefore, we need to locate that icon file in our Moodle server. Follow these steps:

1. Locate where Moodle is installed, as shown in the following screenshot:

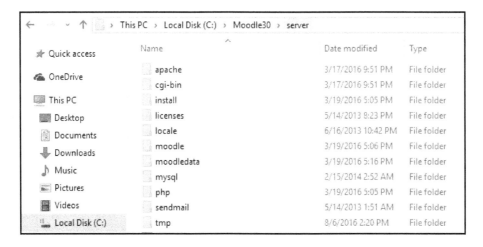

2. Within the server, click on `Moodle\mod\quiz\pix`.

3. The following files appear within the `pix` folder, as shown in the following screenshot:

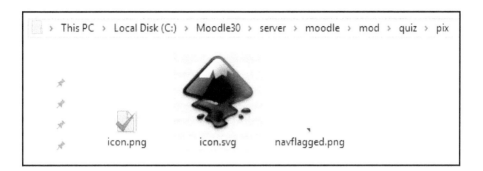

> This PC > Local Disk (C:) > Moodle30 > server > moodle > mod > quiz > pix
>
> icon.png   icon.svg   navflagged.png

We have just located the file that we need to customize. There are two files showing the same image with a different file extension. We need to modify the `.svg` as well as the `.png` since some browsers work with `.png` files while others work with `.svg` ones. If we do not change both files, the icon will not change in the Moodle course.

Downloading Inkscape

In order to edit or customize `.svg` we need to work with Inkscape. Inkscape is a high-quality vector graphics software program which runs on Windows, Mac OS X, and GNU/Linux. We can use Inkscape to create a wide variety of graphics. It can import and export various file formats, including SVG and PNG. Furthermore, it is a free and open source.

We can modify the SVG file and afterwards export it as a PNG file because we need the same icon in a format usable by the software program. We can do it using Inkscape, as was mentioned before. PNG is an open image format that has lossless compression because the images are small in size.

Furthermore, Inkscape is free and open source software and we can download it from the following website: `https://inkscape.org/en/download/`. Depending on the OS that you work with, click on the desired icon, as shown in the following screenshot:

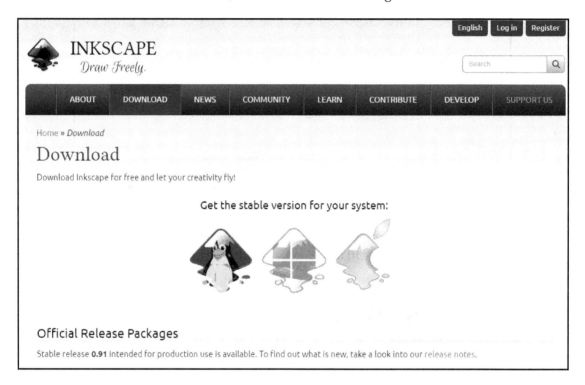

 Follow the installation wizard to finish the installation of Inkscape.

Editing an SVG file

We will work with Inkscape, which we have previously mentioned. So we run said software and we can edit the SVG of the quiz which is the one that we will change in Moodle on-premises. We can also modify other icons. We will use the drawing options in Inkscape to create the desired icon.

Another possibility is to render some parts of it. When we think of rendering parts of vector graphics, we mean that we are going to use a part of a drawing that we have designed. Therefore, we will not use all the shapes in the file; we will save some of them and select them before exporting them. The aim is to transform the selection of a bitmap.

Run the Inkscape software and follow these steps:

1. Click on **File** | **Open**.
2. Look for the file to open (the quiz icon saved as `.svg`) and click on the file.
3. Click on **Open**, as shown in the following screenshot:

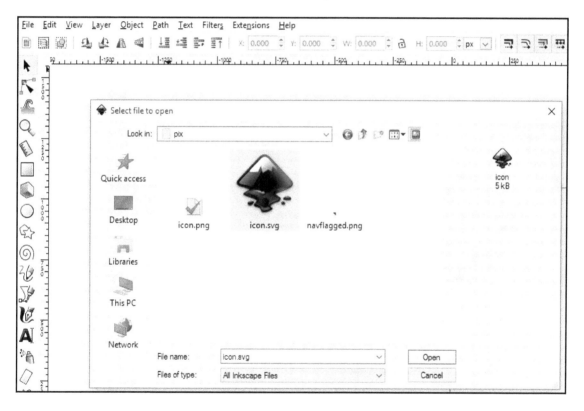

4. Before making any changes to the file, save the file with another name, in order to work with a copy of the original file.
5. Click on **File** | **Save as,** complete the **File name** block, and click on **Save**.

6. Click on the smallest tick of the file, as shown in the following screenshot:

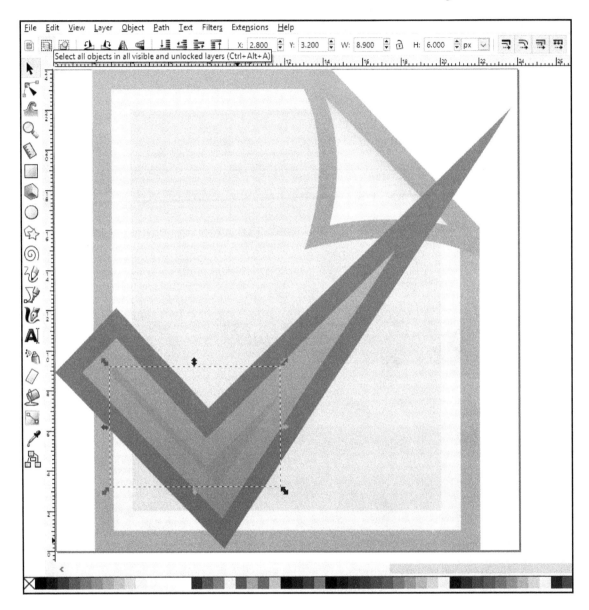

7. Click on any of the colors shown in the palette underneath. For instance, **red**, as shown in the following screenshot:

8. Repeat the same process for the other parts of the SVG.

9. The new SVG is shown in the following screenshot:

10. Click on **File** | **Save**, in order to keep the changes that we have made to the SVG file.

We have just changed the colors of the SVG file. We have made a copy of the original file in case we need to use it. We have to replace this file in the Moodle course, but we have to create a `.png` file as well and replace the one that we have in the Moodle course.

Converting SVG files to PNG files

We have just edited an SVG file but there are two types of files in Moodle. The type of file that Moodle is going to display depends on the web browser or the device that we use. That is to say, it will show either the PNG or the SVG. Thus, what we need to do is to have two identical files with different file extensions.

This transformation process has to be done with Inkscape software and we will convert the SVG to a bitmap image, in other words, we will convert the SVG file to PNG. Follow these steps in order to do it:

1. Click on **File** | **Export PNG Image...**, as shown in the following screenshot:

2. An information block appears on the right-hand side of the margin displaying information for the file, as shown in the following screenshot:

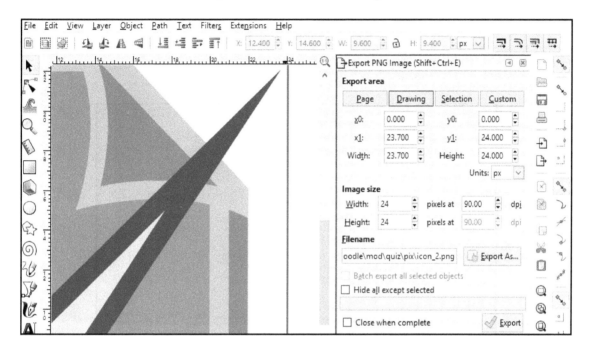

Within the block, the image size appears which reads: Width 24 pixels and Height 24 pixels. We need to check the number of pixels of the original PNG file in order to compare them to check that they are the same size. We cannot add an image with a different number of pixels.

3. Click on **Export**.

Another option is to use free online editing software such as **ImageBot**. We can use it directly from the web browser at `http://www.flamingtext.com/imagebot/editor`. We can upload the file and save it as PNG, as we have done with Inkscape.

Checking the properties of the PNG file

We have edited the SVG file and we have exported it as a PNG. Therefore, we have to check in order to be sure that the number of pixels is the same as the original file. In the example, the number of pixels has not changed since we have only changed the color.

We have to make sure that they are the same size, especially if you alter the file rendering or customize the vector graphic in a different way. We have to work with the original file and the new one; the one that we have edited. Follow these steps in order to do it:

1. Look for the original file and right-click on it.
2. Click on **Properties**.
3. Click on **Details**, as shown in the following screenshot:

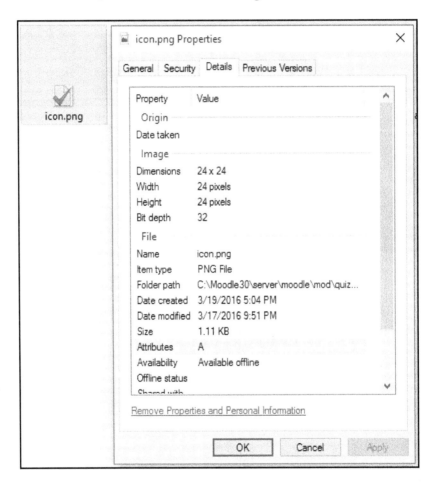

4. The details show that the image has **Width 24 pixels** and **Height 24 pixels**.
5. Click **OK**.

6. Click on the file that we have just edited, even though it was checked in Inkscape for the same number of pixels.
7. Right-click on the file.
8. Click on **Properties**.
9. Click on **Details**, as shown in the following screenshot:

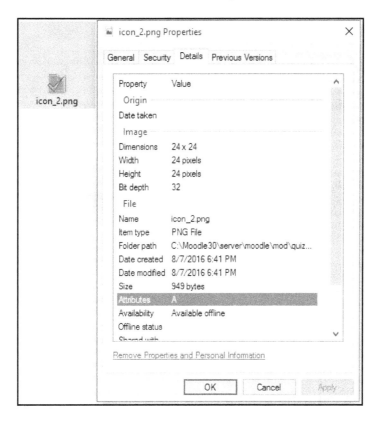

10. The details show that the image has **Width 24 pixels** and **Height 24 pixels**.
11. Click **OK**.

 Both files have the same number of pixels, so we can change them and add the new one to Moodle on-premises.

Replacing the SVG file

It is time to start replacing the files in order to see how the icon changes in Moodle on-premises in further steps. We need to replace files to see this change. We will have to make copies of files and rename files. In this step, we will replace the SVG file.

We have already made a copy of the original file in order to keep it. What we have to do is to rename the edited file as the original so that Moodle changes the file.

Therefore, we will make another copy of the original file and rename the edited file as the original. In order to do it, follow these steps:

1. Look for the original SVG file.
2. Right-click on it and click on **Copy**, as shown in the following screenshot:

3. Right-click and click on **Paste**. We have just made the copy of the original icon.
4. The following icons appear, as shown in the following screenshot:

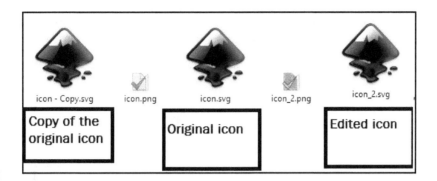

 The screenshot shows three SVG files. From left to right the copies that we have just made of the original icon appear. The original icon and the edited icon. We have to rename the edited icon as the original one because that one is the file that Moodle on-premises uses to display.

5. Delete the original icon. right-click on it and click on **Delete**.
6. Right-click on the edited icon. Click on **Rename**.
7. Write the name of the original icon, as shown in the following screenshot:

Replacing the PNG file

We have just replaced the SVG file and it is time to replace the PNG. We need to change both of them because some web browsers use the PNG file while others use SVG. Therefore, we have to follow the steps that we have followed previously, but in this case with the PNG file. Follow these steps:

1. Look for the original PNG file.
2. Right-click on it and click on **Copy**.

3. Right-click and click on **Paste**. We have just made the copy of the original icon.
4. The following icons appear, as shown in the following screenshot:

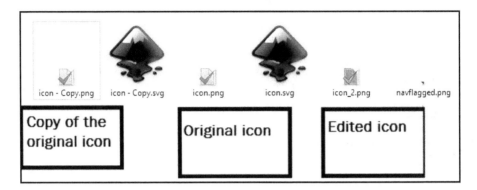

 The screenshot shows three PNG files. From left to right the copies that we have just made of the original icon appear. The original icon and the edited icon. We have to rename the edited icon as the original one because that one is the file that Moodle on-premises uses to display.

4. Delete the original icon. Right-click on it and click on **Delete**.
5. Right-click on the edited icon. Click on **Rename**.
6. Write the name of the original icon, as shown in the following screenshot:

Testing the new icon in Moodle on-premises

We have followed several steps in order to modify an icon in Moodle on-premises, so it is time to test if all the steps that we have performed are correct and we can see the new icon when we add an activity or resource. Follow these steps:

1. Log into Moodle on-premises.
2. Enter the course to add an activity or resource.
3. Click **Turn editing on**.
4. Click **Add an activity or resource** and it looks as shown in the following screenshot:

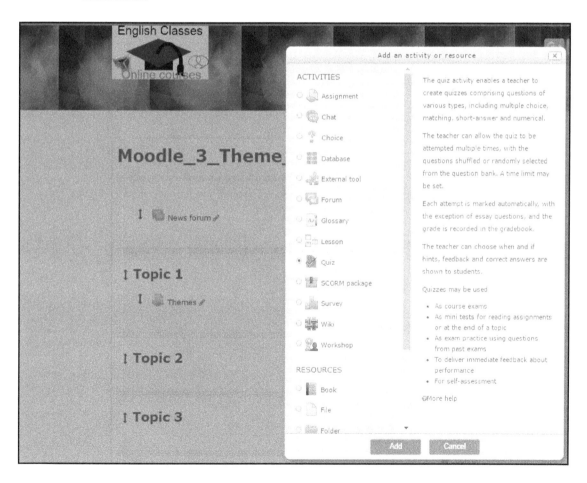

The quiz icon is the one that we have already modified. It is shown in the following screenshots:

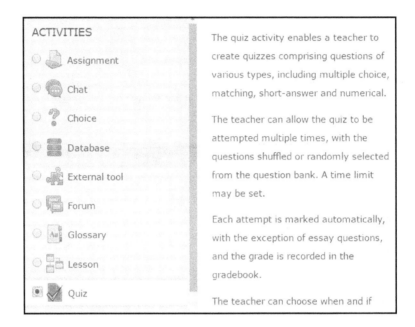

Locating Add an activity or resource icons in our Moodle on-premises

We have just modified a quiz icon and we need to find the other icons in our Moodle on-premises. We can also render parts of icons in order to modify them as we desire. Therefore, we need to find where they are so that we can edit them.

We enter our Moodle on-premises, and after logging in, we enter the desired course and click on **Add an activity or resource**. Under **Activities**, the following activities appear, as shown in the following screenshot:

We can find the icon of the assignment in the following path:
`Moodle\server\moodle\mod\assignment\pix`. The following icons appear, as shown in the following screenshot:

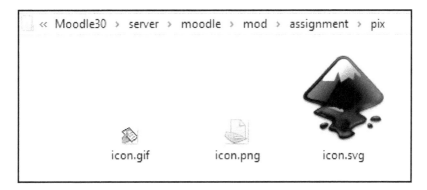

In this case, three different bitmap images appear, that is to say, we have the icons saved with three different extensions: `.gif`, `.png`, and `.svg`. Previously, we have converted the SVG into PNG using Inkscape. We can convert an SVG to a GIF using Inkscape, but we can use other software to do it, such as Paint for Windows users and Preview for Mac OS X users. Therefore, when modifying an icon for an assignment we need to do it in three different formats.

In order to edit the icon of a chat activity, we can find the icon following the same path as before. The only difference is that within mod we click on **Chat** and we can also find three different icon files. They are shown in the following screenshot:

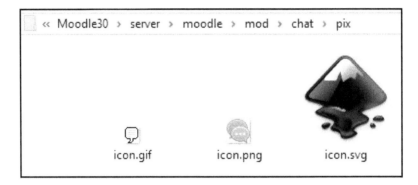

We could keep on adding the path and screenshots of where to find the icons, but that is not the idea of the book. To sum up, we can find the icons within the mod folder, in this folder, we can find the activities, and within the activities, there is a `pix` folder where we can find the icons. In some cases, there are only two icons and in others, there are three icons. It is advisable to save the icon to be used in the three different file extensions.

Within the `mod` folder, these are the files of Moodle on-premises activities. Within them, we can find a `pix` folder containing the icons to edit. It is shown in the following screenshot:

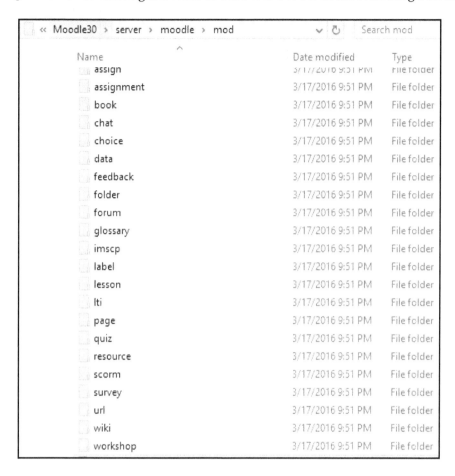

Rendering parts of icons

We have found where the icons of the **Add an activity or resource** are placed on the server. It is time to render part of an icon and to check how it changes in Moodle on-premises. We will work with the `forum` because in this example we will modify two icons. Therefore, in order to check which icons we are working with, we will add a `forum` activity in Moodle on-premises. After adding the activity, we will add a post to the `forum` and this is the result. We will focus on the icons that we will render, they are shown in the following screenshot:

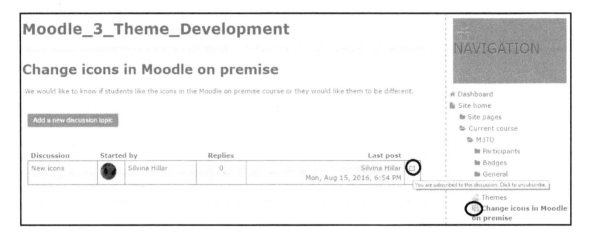

The icons that are circled are the ones that we are going to change. Therefore, these are the steps that we have to follow:

1. Locate the icons. They are in the following path:
   `Moodle30\server\moodle\mod\forum\pix`, as shown in the following screenshot:

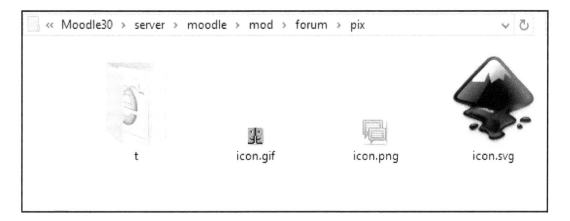

2. Click on the **t** folder. These are the icons that are in the folder and will be rendered, as shown in the following screenshot:

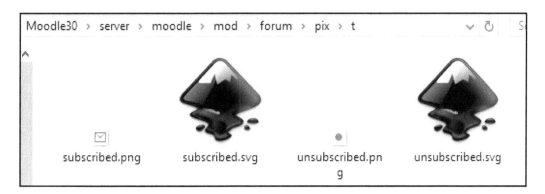

 We have just located the icons that we will render parts of, therefore it is time to work with them. First of all, as we have already done before, we will run Inkscape and open the file to work with.

3. Run Inkscape.
4. Open `icon.svg` within the `pix` folder.

5. Click on **File** | **Save a copy** and write a name for the file.

6. Click on a part of the dialogue cloud, as shown in the following screenshot:

7. Click on delete.
8. Repeat the same process for the other dialogue cloud.

9. Click on the icon to Create and edit text objects, as shown in the following screenshot:

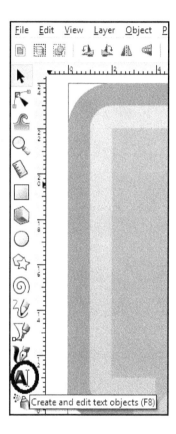

10. Choose the font and size of the letter.
11. Write the word forum inside the dialogue clouds.

12. Click on the Select and transform objects icon and move the word forum into the desired place, it is shown in the following screenshot:

13. Replace both the SVG and the PNG file in the `pix` folder.

14. Run Moodle on-premises, the changes are shown in the following screenshots:

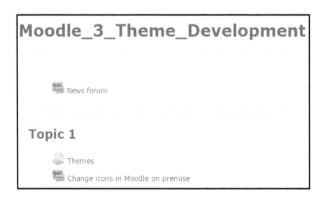

This image shows how the icon looks in the Moodle course.

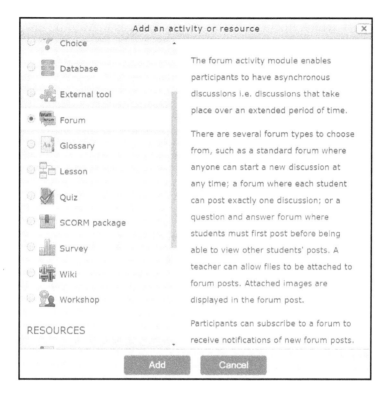

This image shows how the icons that we have just modified appear when we want to add an activity or resource.

This image shows how the modified icon of a forum looks when we click on it to add it.

Test your knowledge

A. We need to modify which file in order to see the changes in Moodle on-premises …

    1. …the `.svg` file.

    2. …the `.png` file.

    3. …both the `.svg` and `.png` files.

B. We have to work with Inkscape …

    1. …to edit a PNG file.

    2. …to edit an SVG file.

    3. …to edit both PNG and SVG files.

C. We need to check the number of pixels of which file that we have edited so that they match the same number of pixels of the original file/files …

    1. …an SVG file.

    2. …a PNG file.

    3. …the SVG and PNG files.

D. We have to rename …

    1. …the edited SVG file as the original only.

    2. …the edited PNG file as the original only.

    3. …both the edited SVG file and the edited PNG file as the original.

E. It is advisable to keep a copy of …

    1. …the edited SVG file.

    2. …the edited PNG file.

    3. …both the original PNG and SVG files.

Summary

In this chapter, we have worked with icons. We have learned how, when, and why we modify icons in order to make the learning experience more effective and achieve learning goals. We have also worked with vector graphics and bitmaps. We have modified an SVG file and exported it as a PNG. We have changed the look and feel of Moodle on-premises course and we personalized the icon. We can also add more images to the icons or edit them in a different way, but we always have to follow the steps that we have taken. We need to make copies of files and replace the edited files with the originals. We may not like how the new icon looks in the Moodle course. Let's keep on personalizing our Moodle on-premises course. The following chapter deals with Optimizing themes for Mobile devices.

7
Optimizing Themes for Mobile Devices

When designing a theme, we must bear in mind that the theme is not only used in desktops/laptops, but also in mobile devices. As regards mobile devices, nowadays we have to consider many of them. It is impossible to test the theme on every mobile device, but it is necessary to do so when we change the look and feel of Moodle on-premises or MoodleCloud. Furthermore, we also need to check the network connectivity, that is to say the time of response and the latency

In order to test how the new theme is displayed and how throttling works in a mobile device, we can use Chrome DevTool's Device Mode, which simulates a wide range of devices and their capabilities. We can emulate sites across different screen sizes as well as resolutions. We can also emulate orientation.

In this chapter, we will focus on mobile devices and how themes look in them. We will customize different mobile devices because we can find it relevant when theming in our Moodle courses. Furthermore, there may be mobile devices that are not shown within Google device mode, and we can add them. New products are available on the market and we can customize the device as well as the resolution and add it. After adding it, we can check what the theme looks like.

In regards to network connectivity, we can limit the internet connection of the device that we are working with and we can simulate how the connectivity would be on such a device. Moreover, we can custom the throttle or we can modify it. We can also check how the theme responds to the connectivity.

Each device has a different **User Experience** (**UX**), which has to generate a reasonable UX for all devices. So in order to achieve this UX, we need to emulate devices as well as its network connection.

In this chapter, we shall:

- Download the Google Chrome web browser
- Enable device mode
- Edit an emulated device
- Add a custom device
- Check network throttling profiles
- Emulate network connectivity

Downloading Google Chrome web browser

In this chapter, we will optimize themes for mobile devices, and in order to do so, we need to check how the Moodle theme that we are designing looks on different devices. It is impossible to have all the devices available on the market and test the Moodle theme on them; therefore, we need to do it through a simulator.

We can simulate mobile devices with Device Mode in Google Chrome, therefore, we need to download Google Chrome web browser in order to use this tool. We can download it from the following website: `https://www.google.com/chrome/`.

Hover the mouse over **DOWNLOAD** and click the desired option, as shown in the following screenshot:

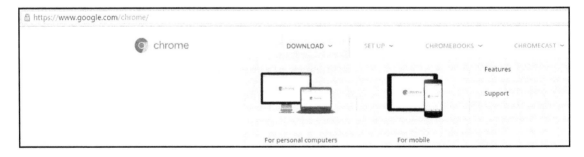

In this example, we are working on a personal computer; therefore, we click on **For personal computers**. Follow the installation wizard in order to complete the installation of the Chrome web browser.

Enabling device mode

We have already installed the Chrome web browser, therefore, we need to run it. After running it, we have to run MoodleCloud or Moodle on-premises on it. Therefore, in this example, we will run MoodleCloud. We will test how it looks on a mobile device. First of all, we will check how we see it in our desktop. Although, the way we see it may differ according to the resolution of the monitor that we have, it will look much different on a mobile device. Follow these steps:

1. Run Google Chrome.
2. Run MoodleCloud or Moodle on-premises and log in.
3. Press the *F12* key.
4. Then the following screen will appear:

5. Click on **Toggle device toolbar**, as shown in the following screenshot:

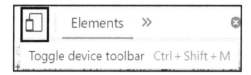

6. Then the following appears on the right-hand side of the margin (it can also appear beneath the screen):

 TIP

On the left-hand side of the page, the simulation of a mobile device appears and it shows the MoodleCloud that we are running on our desktop on a mobile device. We can see that the theme looks quite different from the one that we have designed. Therefore, we can make the necessary changes to the theme to design a look and feel according to the needs of a mobile device. For instance, in this case, the description of the courses may be too long and if they were shorter, the entire course would be displayed.

7. When hovering the mouse over the simulated device, you can find all the information within the MoodleCloud course. The columns that were on both sides are after the courses.

7. The following screenshots compare and contrast MoodleCloud on a desktop and MoodleCloud on a mobile device:

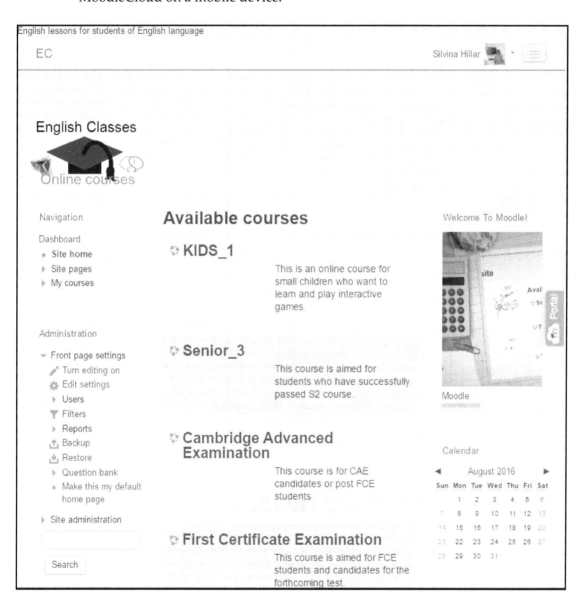

The left-hand side column and the right-hand side column were placed downwards, therefore, when scrolling down we will find them:

Editing an emulated device

There are many mobile devices on the market, therefore, we may customize our simulator for a specific device or we may explore all the options to check how the theme looks. Besides, we may need to make some improvements or change the look and feel according to the way it looks on certain mobile devices.

Follow these steps in order to customize a device:

1. Run Google Chrome.
2. Run MoodleCloud or Moodle on-premises and log in.
3. Press the *F12* key.
4. Once you have enabled **Toggle device toolbar**, go to the left-hand side of the screen where we can find the simulated device.
5. Click on the downwards arrow next to **Responsive**, as shown in the following screenshot:

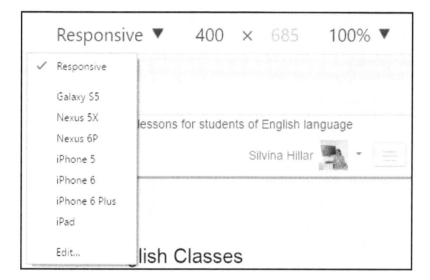

6. A pop-up menu will appear, as shown in the previous screenshot.
7. Click on **Edit...**.
8. On the right-hand side, a list of emulated devices will appear, as shown in the following screenshot:

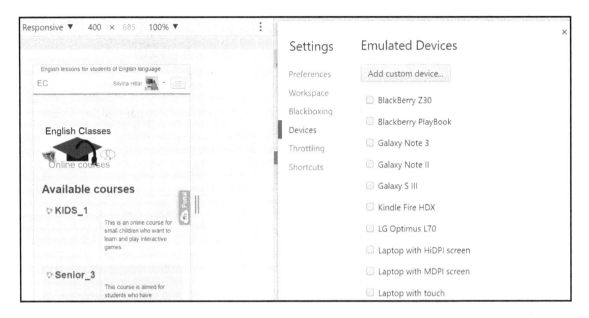

9. Then a list of mobile devices will appear.
10. Scroll downwards and a list of ticked mobile devices (left screenshot) will appear which are the same in the drop-down menu under **Responsive** (right screenshot). It is shown in the following screenshots:

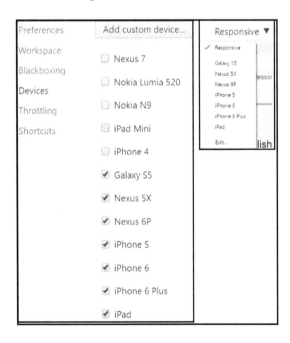

Adding a custom device

Considering the fact that there are new devices and we may not know all of them, we can also add a custom device. We need to check how the theme looks on several devices or we need to check a certain device, which does not appear in the list shown in the previous example, therefore, we need to customize a device. In this example, we can explore a device running on Android such as **BLU RH1**.

Before customizing the device, we need to check some details, so we will enter the official website at `http://bluproducts.com/r1-hd/` and get the specification. It is shown in the following screenshot:

After checking the specification of the new device, we do not close that tab and follow these steps:

1. Run Google Chrome.
2. Run MoodleCloud or Moodle on-premises and log in.
3. Press the *F12* key.

4. Once you have enabled **Toggle device toolbar**, go to the left-hand side of the screen where we can find the simulated device.
5. Click on the downwards arrow next to **Responsive**.
6. Click on **Edit....**.
7. Click on **Add custom device**, as shown in the following screenshot:

8. Some blocks will appear that we need to complete, as shown in the following screenshot:

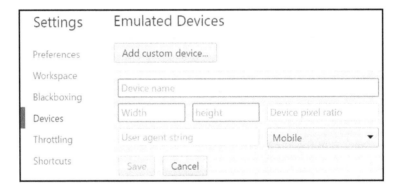

9. Complete the **Device name** block, writing the name of the device.
10. Complete the **Width** and **height** blocks. The information is provided on the website under **Display HD 720×1280**.

11. After completing the necessary data, click on **Save**, as shown in the following screenshot:

12. The device appears under **Emulated Devices**, as shown in the following screenshot:

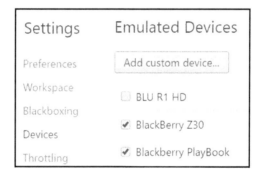

13. Click on **BLU R1 HD**; the device that has just been customized.

14. Click on the cross on the top right-hand side margin, as shown in the following screenshot:

15. On the left-hand side of the screen, click on **Responsive**.

16. A drop-down menu will appear, click on **BLU R1 HD**, as shown in the following screenshot:

17. The emulated device is shown in the following screenshot:

 We can emulate the rotation of the device. Click on the **Rotate** icon and we can see how Moodle is shown in landscape orientation. The first screenshot shows the Rotate icon. The second screenshot shows the landscape orientation of Moodle:

 Whenever we check the theme on mobile devices, we must check rotation as well since the theme may look better here. Moreover, we can eliminate some columns in order to avoid them and see the central part of the theme. It will all depend on the target audience of the Moodle course. Where do the students use it more frequently? After answering that question, we need to work out the columns.

Checking network throttling profiles

When emulating a device, we not only check how the theme looks, but we also need to check network-throttling profiles. We can do it using **Google DevTools** as well. We can also custom throttles in case we want to add more information.

When we throttle, we limit the speed and response time. Furthermore, we can also see how throttling works while emulating the device. We can see how the network connectivity works and we can select the items that we want to test. Here are some steps that we have to follow:

1. Run Google Chrome.
2. Run MoodleCloud or Moodle on-premises and log in.
3. Press the *F12* key.

4. Click on the **Toggle device toolbar** icon.
5. Click on the downwards arrow under **Responsive**.
6. Choose the device to simulate.
7. Click on **Edit**, as shown in the following screenshot:

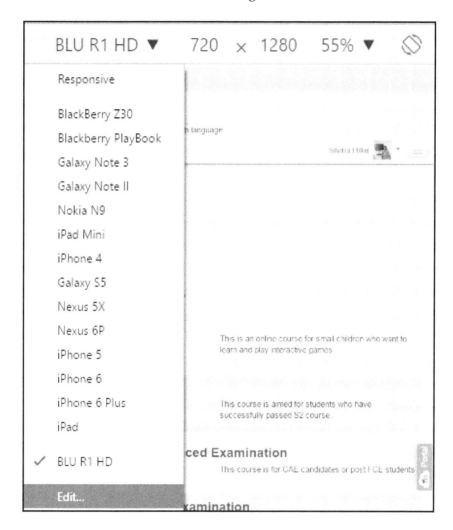

8. Under **Settings**, click on **Throttling**, as shown in the following screenshot:

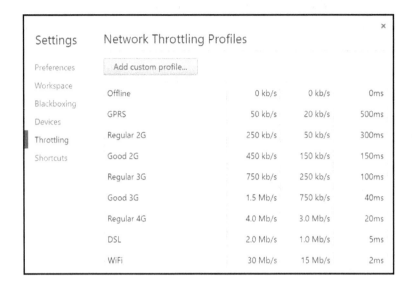

A chart appears, which shows the default conditions. The first column shows the download speed, the second column shows the upload speed, and the third column shows the latency.

kb/s stands for kilobyte per second.

Mb/s stands for megabyte per second.

ms stands for millisecond.

9. Click on **Add custom profile...** to add another item in the previous chart, as shown in the following screenshot:

10. Complete the **Profile Name** block, if desired, complete the **Download**, **Upload**, and **Latency** blocks.

11. After completing the blocks, click on **Add**, as shown in the following screenshot:

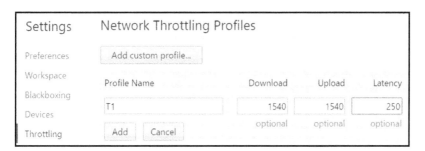

12. The new item appears, as shown in the following screenshot:

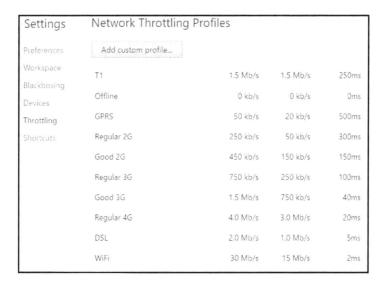

When hovering the mouse over **T1** (the item which was recently added) the Edit or Remove icons appear. It means that we can either edit or delete the information; it is shown in the following screenshot:

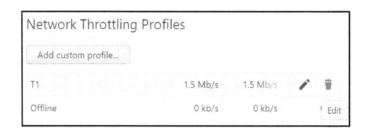

Emulating network connectivity

Throughout this chapter, we have emulated different devices in order to check how our theme works. As it is online software and we need an Internet connection, the emulation is not going to be accurate enough, but we will have a close idea for how it works. We will limit the network connectivity on our desktop or laptop device (among others) in order to emulate network connectivity on a chosen device. Here are the steps that we have to follow:

1. Run Google Chrome.
2. Run MoodleCloud or Moodle on-premises and log in.
3. Press the *F12* Key.
4. Click on **Toggle device toolbar**.
5. On the right-hand side of the screen, click on **Network**, as shown in the following screenshot:

6. Click on **No throttling**.
7. A drop-down menu will appear and you need to click on the desired speed, for example, **Regular 4G**, as shown in the following screenshot:

8. A warning icon will appear next to **Network**, showing that there is a limit on the speed connection (in this example, working as **Regular 4G**), as shown in the following screenshot:

9. Click on any course in the emulated device on the left-hand side of the screen.

10. On the right-hand side of the screen, a screen appears showing how network connectivity works in detail. This example shows all the items uploading on the right-hand side, as shown in the following screenshot:

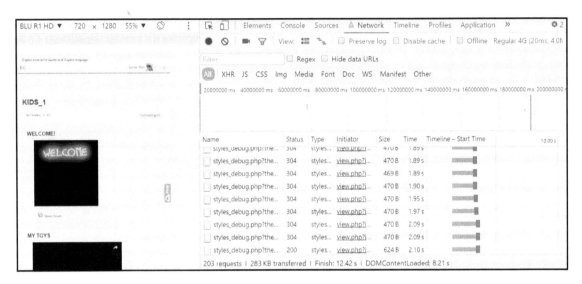

11. Click on **Font** to check only its connectivity, as shown in the following screenshot:

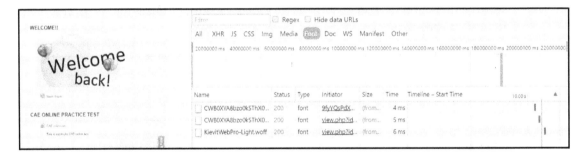

In the last screenshot, there appears how the font downloads in the mobile device on the right-hand side of the screen.

In the previous screenshot, the photos fonts among other items are shown as they download. The information appears on the right-hand side of the screen. We can choose what we want to test according to the type of theme that we want to design.

Test your knowledge

A. We can enable Device Mode in Google Chrome by …

    1. …pressing the *F12* key and clicking on the Toggle Device Toolbar icon.

    2. …pressing the *F11* key and clicking on the Toggle Device Toolbar icon.

    3. …pressing the *F2* key and clicking on the Toggle Device Toolbar icon.

B. We can edit an emulated device by selecting …

    1. …blackboxing.

    2. …devices.

    3. …throttling.

C. In order to add a custom device, we need to complete …

    1. …the device's name block only.

    2. …the device's name, width, and height blocks without exception.

    3. …the width and height blocks and the device's name appear automatically.

D. When we throttle a network connectivity for the device …

    1. …we simulate the Internet speed of the mobile device.

    2. …we emulate the exact device.

    3. …we limit the internet speed of the device that we are using, but we can't emulate the internet speed of the mobile device.

E. When we emulate network connectivity, we can …

    1. …choose what we need to emulate.

    2. …emulate a set of default items.

    3. …emulate fonts only.

Summary

In this chapter, we have worked with emulators for mobile devices, we have also checked internet connectivity and we have learned how to modify, edit, and customize some of these options. We have worked with Google DevTools, which is an online emulator, and we can easily learn how to work with a mobile device from either our desktop or laptop. Moreover, we have emulated network connectivity to check how the theme downloads on a mobile, custom device and optimize for all connection speeds.

We can customizing not only the device, but also its connectivity. When throttling the connectivity, we can see the speed. In the next chapter, we will continue theming our Moodle course. In the following chapter, we will deal with *Exploring Layouts*.

8
Exploring Layouts

Whenever we design a Moodle course, we have to bear in mind the target audience. That is the reason why there are so many themes available to download in order to align with the myriad goals or needs of the users. In this chapter, we will explore all the layouts available at the time of writing, and the different styles that we can apply to them in order to adjust the theme to our audience.

There are some themes that happen to be much more customizable than others; in other words, changing the skin, look, and feel, of our course is simpler in some themes than others. Therefore, in order to cater to our needs, we need to explore the themes and their profile in order to decide which one we shall customize our Moodle course with.

There are themes suitable for academic as well as corporate usage; we can change the look and feel in order to modify them a little bit and adapt them to the situation in which we will use them. Moreover, there are themes that are suitable for kids or modern students; in such cases, we will just add multimedia condiments to these themes and a few changes in order to make them more appealing to these target audiences.

Higher education, such as universities, or corporations who would like to set courses for employees, do have themes tailored for them; in such cases, the suitable themes are two columns or themes with some special condiments and favorable for our target audience. It all depends on what we are looking for when designing a course, and everything is adaptable to whatever we have in mind when customizing our Moodle on-premises course.

We can design a Moodle on-premises course that's similar to a website used for modern e-learning. The more we explore the available themes, the more we can think how to change it! Exploring themes is an important task to bear in mind before designing the course.

Taking into consideration that we can use Moodle on-premises for personal use or small educational establishments, we can find a theme for that as well. Creating courses can be possible for a specific, small audience; therefore, we do have a theme for this audience.

Moodle on-premises is to be used in this chapter since MoodleCloud does not allow us to explore the different themes available in the plugin. We have already covered the themes that are available in MoodleCloud at the time of writing in earlier chapters.

The only theme that we will not be working with in this chapter is essential since we have been dealing with it in the previous chapters, and also because it is the number one theme used and downloaded. The theme is intended to make the site look as little like Moodle as possible, bearing in mind that the theme is useful as a company homepage and not as a course list per se .

In this chapter, we shall cover the following topics:

- Exploring themes suitable for academic use
- Exploring themes suitable for corporations, companies, and professionals
- Exploring themes for personal use
- Exploring two-column themes
- Exploring website themes
- Exploring miscellaneous themes
- Comparing and contrasting all the themes

Exploring themes suitable for academic use

There are several themes for Moodle 3.0 as well as for 3.1 for academic use at the time of writing, so we will explore them. We will focus on the themes available for Moodle versions 3.0 and 3.1, although there are plenty of other themes which work with earlier versions of Moodle. When talking about academic use, we mean that we can use them at different levels of education, as well as in institutes. There are condiments that we can add to the themes in order to adapt them to their location.

In order to explore Moodle themes, we need to go to the following website: `https://moodle.org/plugins/browse.php?list=category&id=3`. On this website are all the themes that we can download for our Moodle on-premises for free; therefore, we will list and explore the ones for academic use.

Contemporary

This is a theme for academic as well as corporate use. It is available for Moodle 3.0 and for earlier Moodle on-premises versions. According to its description, it is a fluid-width, three-column theme. It is also customizable. Follow these steps to download the **Contemporary** theme:

1. Click on **Contemporary**, as shown in the following screenshot:

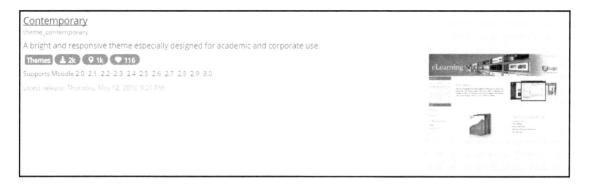

2. After clicking on **Contemporary**, more information appears about the theme.
3. Click on **Versions**.
4. We can download the theme according to the Moodle version that we are using.
5. Click on **Download**, as shown in the following screenshot:

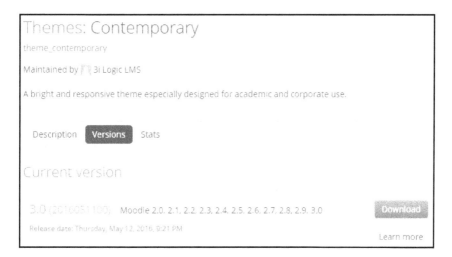

6. Copy and paste the `Contemporary` folder in the theme directory of the Moodle on-premises.
7. Open the browser.
8. Run Moodle on-premises.
9. Click on **Upgrade Moodle database now**, as shown in the following screenshot:

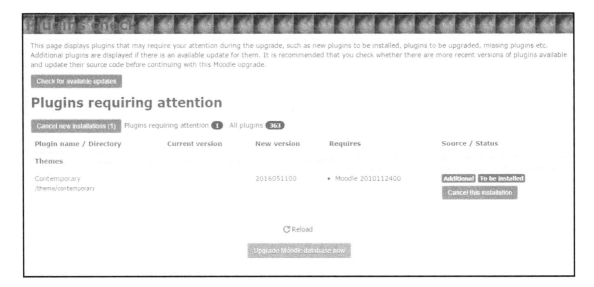

10. Click on **Continue**, as shown in the following screenshot:

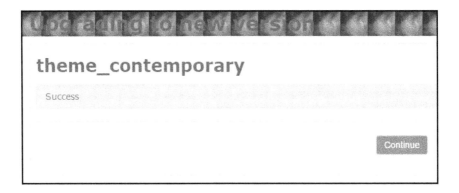

11. Customize the setting of **Contemporary**. Scroll down the page and click on **Save changes**.

12. Navigate to **Site Administration** | **Appearance** | **Themes** | **Theme selector**.

13. Click on **Change theme**, as shown in the following screenshot:

14. Click on **Use theme**, as shown in the following screenshot:

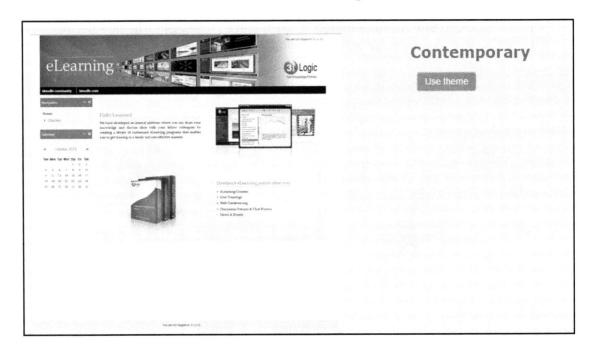

15. Click on **Continue**, as shown in the following screenshot:

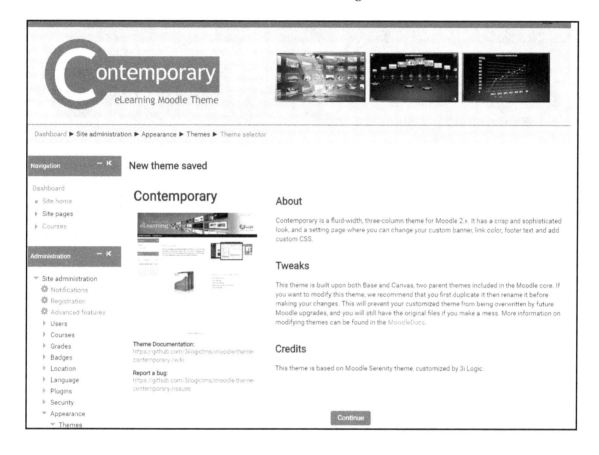

16. The Moodle on-premises course looks as shown in the following screenshot:

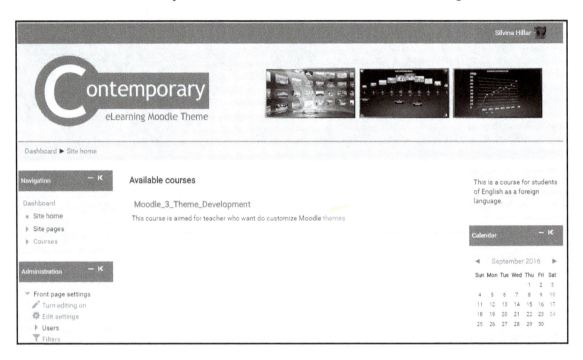

In this example, we have installed an academic theme and have kept the courses that we had in the previous theme because we have saved the changes. There are other academic themes that we can use in Moodle 3.0 or Moodle 3.1. In order to install any of the following themes, just follow the previous steps.

Aardvark

Aardvark is a theme for modern students; therefore, it means that it is related to academic use. It is available for both Moodle 3.0 and Moodle 3.1 as well as other previous Moodle versions. We can download it from `https://moodle.org/plugins/theme_aardvark`, as shown in the following screenshot:

Academi

Academi is also an academic theme. It has many interesting features, such as responsive layout, browser compatibility, and a front page slideshow. Apart from that, we can customize CSS, the logo, and the menu. Furthermore, there are front page course blocks, category blocks, and an info block on the footer. We can configure social media links on the footer as well. We can manage slider images, text description, copyrights, contents, and contact information. Plenty of things can be done with Academi. We can download it from `https://moodle.org/plugins/theme_academi`, as shown in the following screenshot:

Adaptable

This is another Academi theme that is highly customizable. There are marketing, footer, and region blocks that can be customized as well. We can customize fonts, colors, and icons. There are plenty of items that are customizable using this theme; one interesting feature is that the My courses list can be organized so that older courses are sub-menu items.

There is also support for a social wall in course format, and mobile settings that give greater control over how the theme looks on mobile devices, which is an important asset to bear in mind in a mobile world!

We can also add a login form in the header on the front page, a favicon uploader, and a background image uploader, among other features. We can download the **Adaptable** theme from `https://moodle.org/plugins/theme_adaptable`, as shown in the following screenshot:

In addition many fields (menus, news items, alerts and help links) can be targeted using custom profile fields, thus it is possible to present different users with different nagivation items and notices.

It is also possible for individual users to customise where they want top menu navigation to appear (disable, home pages only, sitewide) using custom profile fields.

Adaptable has a lot of settings and may seem daunting at first, our advice is to simply install with the default settings and play with it afterwards.

With a little time you should be able to setup an attractive Moodle site with a high degree of individuality without without knowing any CSS.

Credits:

- Adaptable is a fork of BCU theme and owes its existence to all those credited on that theme
- Adaptable development was driven by 3Bits E-Learning Solutions and Coventry University
- Persistence of Bootstrap Alerts provided by Justin Hunt in between mowing lawns and brokering cease fires (see his Moodle Services page)
- Ideas on Social Wall support provided by Chris Kenniburg
- Help with renderers and other tricky stuff provided by Mary Evans and Gareth J Barnard
- Additional support provided by New School Learning

eGuru

eGuru is another theme that belongs to the category of Academi. It is defined as an ultra-responsive Moodle theme with a multi-color pattern. It works on all devices and all browsers and it is a suitable choice for educational establishments. It is available for Moodle 3 as well as for earlier versions of Moodle. It is customizable in many ways (login page, CSS, logo for header and footer, menu, and so on).

Furthermore, it has a responsive layout and a multilingual theme. We can also configure social media links on the footer and manage slider images, text, hyperlink, contents, and contact information. It can be downloaded from `https://moodle.org/plugins/theme_egu ru`, as shown in the following screenshot:

Pioneer

Pioneer is another Academi theme, which has many features in the theme itself and plenty of other features for both teachers and students. As regards the features of the theme, it has plenty of customizations available, such as colors, logo, site header image, and course header images, among others. It also has site alerts, front page tab display, social icons, and social course format integration. There are plenty of other options available to change the look and feel of this Academi theme.

Concerning the teacher features, the main advantage is that the turn editing button is always visible on the page. We can customize full-width header images for course searching and control the **My courses** dropdown. On the other hand, students' features include an activity completion visual display, a total course grade visual display, and a course grade book slider, among other features. We can download Pioneer from `https://moodle.org/plugins/theme_pioneer`, as shown in the following screenshot:

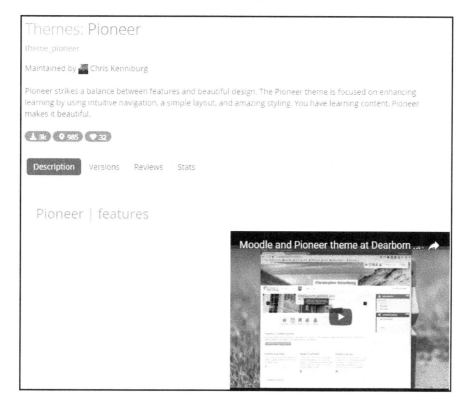

Dynamic

Dynamic belongs to the academic group available for Moodle 3, as well as for earlier versions. It is a dynamic, fluid-width, three-column theme. It is also similar to a website. It includes a basic settings page where you can change the logo, tag line, footer, and custom CSS. It works on mobile devices. It can be downloaded from `https://moodle.org/plugins/theme_dynamic`, as shown in the following screenshot:

Themes: Dynamic

theme_dynamic

Maintained by 3i Logic LMS

A lively responsive theme with sections on the homepage, especially suitable for academic and personal use.

765   856   28

Eduhub

Eduhub is a fantastic theme for educational purposes; there are some features that can be controlled by its settings page. We can also change the image on the front page as well as the banner text. We can customize marketing blocks, the theme color, and the footer image. It works on Moodle 3 and 3.1, as well as earlier Moodle versions. It can be downloaded from `https://moodle.org/plugins/pluginversions.php?plugin=theme_eduhub`, as shown in the following screenshot:

Snap

Snap is a Moodle theme within the academic group. It enables teachers to create modern, engaging **UXs (User Experiences)** on the Web. The layout focuses on the learning activities and content. It is available on desktops and mobile devices. It could be also suitable for professional environments. It can be downloaded from `https://moodle.org/plugins/theme_snap`, as shown in the following screenshot:

Sharp

Sharp is an academic theme, and it can also be used for personal and professional use. It is a two-column, fluid-width theme. We can customize menus, it has a variety of colors, and it includes a basic settings page so that it can be customized. It works in Moodle 3 and earlier versions. It can be downloaded from `https://moodle.org/plugins/theme_sharp`, as shown in the following screenshot:

Klass

This is a modern, responsive Moodle theme that is suitable for e-learning websites. It is suitable for schools as well as for universities. It also works on desktops and mobile devices. It is suitable for Moodle 3 as well as earlier versions of Moodle. We can download **Klass** from `https://moodle.org/plugins/pluginversions.php?plugin=theme_klass`:

Exploring themes suitable for corporations, companies, and professionals

There are some themes that we listed in the previous section that are also suitable for entrepreneurs; therefore, we will just name them in order to keep on exploring more themes in this category. These are the themes that we have just explored that are suitable for entrepreneurs: Essential, Contemporary, Adaptable, and Sharp.

There are more themes that have not been explored yet, so let's explore them and widen the possibility of enhancing our Moodle courses

Rocket

Rocket is a professional, fixed-width theme that is customizable, so we can avoid our Moodle site looking so Moodley. It has plenty of features, such as setting up a logo and the custom menu, which are controlled in the settings. It is available for Moodle 3 as well as for earlier versions. It can be downloaded from `https://moodle.org/plugins/pluginversions.php?plugin=theme_rocket`, as shown in the following screenshot:

Shoehorn

Shoehorn is a clean and professional theme that has many innovative features, such as block regions and a compact navigation bar option, among others. It also has a dynamic and customizable footer menu, as well as dynamic social icons. It has some incredible characteristics that make this theme suitable for professional use. We can download this theme from the following website: `https://moodle.org/plugins/pluginversions.php?plugin=theme_shoehorn`. It is available for Moodle 3.1 and Moodle 3, as well as earlier Moodle versions.

We will download the Shoehorn theme and change the theme in our Moodle on-premises course so that we have a professional theme. We will have to follow the installation wizard as well as the steps mentioned earlier in this chapter. The Moodle course looks as shown in the following screenshot after the theme is applied:

Exploring themes for personal use

We have already explored these themes earlier in this chapter because there are only two themes available at the time of writing. These themes are Dynamic and Sharp. In order to explore them a little bit more, we will show a screenshot of our Moodle course using Sharp.

Sharp

We explained this theme earlier in this chapter since it is also a theme that can be used for professional and academic use. Therefore, we can take a look at our Moodle course dressed in this theme. In order to change the theme of our Moodle course we need to follow the steps that were described earlier in this chapter, as well as the installation wizard. The Moodle on-premises course looks as shown in the following screenshot:

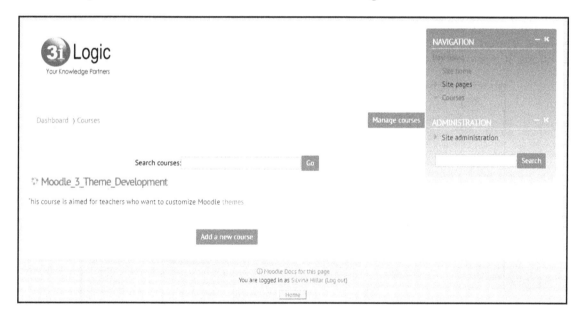

Exploring two-column themes

There are a few two-column themes, and we have already explored some of them. The Two-column themes are **Adaptable** and **Sharp,** which we've explored in the previous sections. In this section, we'll explore **Elegance**. When theming our Moodle on-premises course, we can choose between three-column or two-column themes. The themes that we have mentioned have two columns, among other features. We will pay special attention to Elegance because we have worked with the other two themes before.

Elegance

Elegance is a beautiful, two-column Moodle theme, which can be customized. The items that we can customize are icons, fonts, quick links, marketing spots, front page content, footer content, colors, user menu, and log in screen. We can download the **Elegance** theme from the following website: https://moodle.org/plugins/pluginversions.php?plugin =theme_elegance. It runs in Moodle 3.1 as well as in Moodle 3.0 and earlier Moodle versions. It is shown in the following screenshot:

Exploring website themes

There are two themes that are based on websites, and one of them has been explored already. The theme that we have been working with throughout the book is **Essential**, which is similar to a home page rather than a Moodle course, and that is the intention of the designer of this theme. The other theme that is similar to a website is **Crisp**. We will explore it in this section.

Crisp

Crisp has several characteristics that make it suitable for designing a more specialized and clean website. It offers a **Lemmon Slider** on the home page. We can upload a favicon and a logo. It has blog support, and course and forum pages are navigable from the home page. It has very interesting features that can make your Moodle course look like a perfect website. **Crisp** is available for Moodle 3 as well as for earlier versions. We can download it from `htt ps://moodle.org/plugins/pluginversions.php?plugin=theme_crisp`, as shown in the following screenshot:

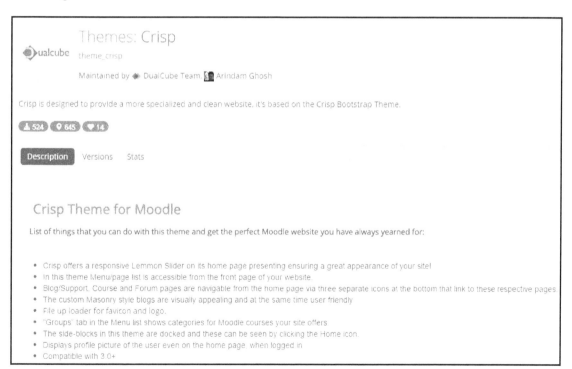

Exploring miscellaneous themes

There are several themes that can be used to change the look and feel of our Moodle course according to what we need; therefore, we will explore miscellaneous themes, which have several categories and might be interesting when designing a specific course. The themes are listed hereinafter, and there is a short description of each one.

Archaius

Archaius can be downloaded from the following website: `https://moodle.org/plugins/theme_archaius`. It has several options to customize, such as social icons, uploading a logo, and the background image, among others. We can also customize the color of the current block tab and the current item in the custom menu. There are other features that can be customized as well, including CSS and JavaScript in the footer. It is available for Moodle 3 and earlier Moodle versions.

Bootstrap

The **Bootstrap** theme does not have much of a description, but it says that it is based on the Bootstrap CSS framework, and it has minimal styling. We can use this theme to create UX-optimized themes. It is available for Moodle 3.1 and Moodle 3, as well as for earlier versions. It can be downloaded from the following website: `https://moodle.org/plugins/pluginversions.php?plugin=theme_bootstrap`.

Roshnilite

Roshnilite is available for Moodle 3.1 and Moodle 3 as well as earlier Moodle versions. It is a beautiful theme and provides customizable sections on the front page through a settings panel. It has dynamic **Masonry** blocks, an automatic course display on the front page, and customizable theme colors and social icons, among other features. It can be downloaded from the following website: `https://moodle.org/plugins/pluginversions.php?plugin` `=theme_roshnilite`.

Campus

Campus is a customizable theme through which we can change the look and feel of the Moodle course. It is fully responsive and it has features such as a slideshow and social icons, among others. We can customize it so that it becomes a perfect Moodle site. It is available for Moodle 3.1 and Moodle 3 as well as earlier versions. It can be downloaded from the following website: `https://moodle.org/plugins/pluginversions.php?plugin =theme_campus`. It is shown in the following screenshot:

Morecandy

Morecandy is a theme based on More, but it has a different look. It is customizable in many ways, and marketing spots can be added to any section of the front page. On the website, `ht tps://moodle.org/plugins/theme_morecandy`, there is an example of HTML code through which we can add two sections to the page.

It is available for Moodle 3.1 and Moodle 3 as well as earlier versions. The following screenshot shows how to customize the front page:

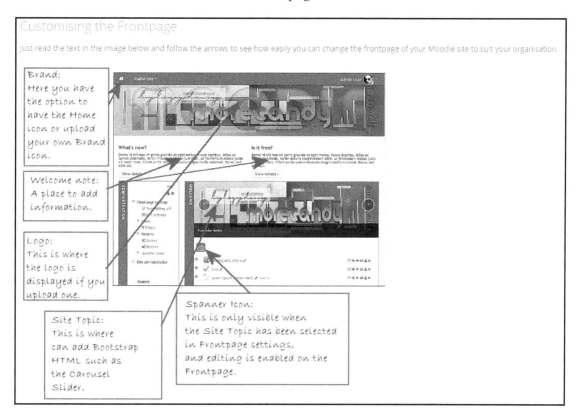

 The screenshot was taken from the website, `https://moodle.org/plugin s/theme_morecandy`, which was previously mentioned.

UIkit

UIkit is a very interactive and visual customizer theme. It has a fully responsive design, as well as many other interesting features, such as login page and navigation menu customization and the ability to only show enrolled courses in combo lists, among other attractive characteristics. It supports Moodle 2.5 to 3.0. It can be downloaded from the following website: `https://moodle.org/plugins/pluginversions.php?plugin=theme_ui kit`. It is shown in the following screenshot:

Aigne

Aigne is suitable for places where there is a slow Internet connection and it improves the rate of loading pages, giving a new look. It is widely customizable since it has more than 100 options to change. Among its interesting features are a personalized logo, slogan, and background logo image, and a contact section with about 30 social network links. It is available for Moodle 3 as well as for earlier versions. It can be downloaded from the following website, `https://moodle.org/plugins/pluginversions.php?plugin=theme_ai gne`:

Flexibase

Flexibase is a Moodle theme whose aim is to provide an experimental format in order to use flexbox CSS layouts. It is customizable in many ways. It is based upon the Bas Brands Bootstrap theme for Bootstrap 3. It is available for Moodle 3.1 and 3 as well as earlier Moodle versions. We can download it from the following website, `https://moodle.org/pl ugins/pluginversions.php?plugin=theme_flexibase`:

Decaf

Decaf's interesting asset is that it has an awesome bar at the top of the screen, from which a menu drops down containing everything in the navigation and settings blocks. It is available for Moodle 3.1 and Moodle 3 as well as for earlier versions. It can be downloaded from the following website, `https://moodle.org/plugins/pluginversions.php?plugin =theme_decaf`:

Afterburner

Afterburner is a theme that was coded for Moodle 2. It is available for this Moodle version as well as for Moodle 3 and Moodle 3.1. It is a three-column, fluid-width theme. We can download it from the website, `https://moodle.org/plugins/pluginversions.php?plugi n=theme_afterburn`:

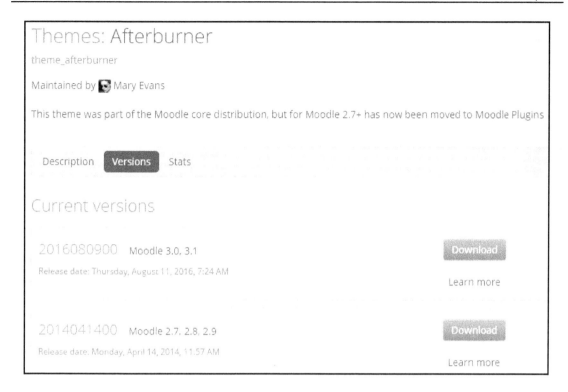

Bootswatch

Bootswatch is available for Moodle 3. It is a child theme, as it inherits its functions and styles from a parent theme. If we download it from the website, `https://moodle.org/plug ins/pluginversions.php?plugin=theme_bootswatch`, we can select a Bootswatch, which is a sub-theme.

We can download a variety of subthemes from `http://bootswatch.com/`, as shown in the following screenshot:

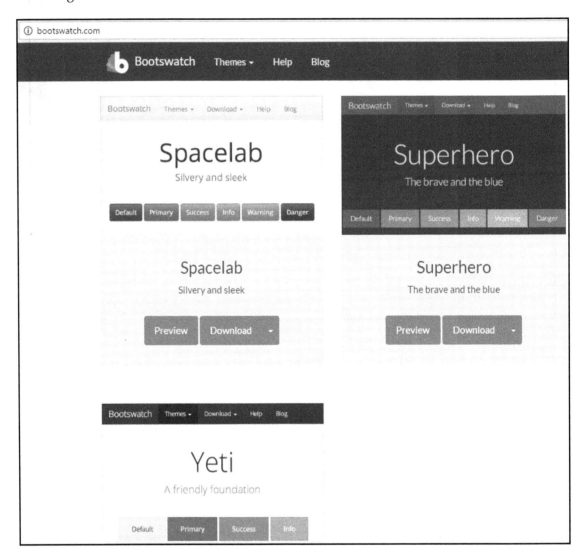

Cerulean

Cerulean is available for Moodle 3 and earlier Moodle versions. It is another child theme, like Bootswatch. We can download it from the website, `https://moodle.org/plugins/plu` `ginversions.php?plugin=theme_cerulean`:

Splash

Splash is available for Moodle 3 and earlier Moodle versions. It is a fluid-width three-column theme. It can be downloaded from the website, `https://moodle.org/plugins/plu` `ginversions.php?plugin=theme_splash`:

Serenity

Serenity is available for Moodle 3.1 and Moodle 3 as well as earlier Moodle versions. It is a fluid-width, three-column theme that can be downloaded from the following website, `http` `s://moodle.org/plugins/pluginversions.php?plugin=theme_serenity`:

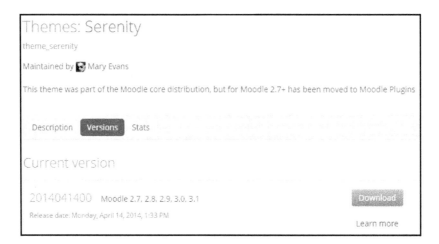

Anomaly

Anomaly is available for Moodle 3.1 and Moodle 3 as well as earlier Moodle versions. It is a fluid-width, three-column theme with round corners, which can be downloaded from the website, `https://moodle.org/plugins/pluginversions.php?plugin=theme_anomaly`:

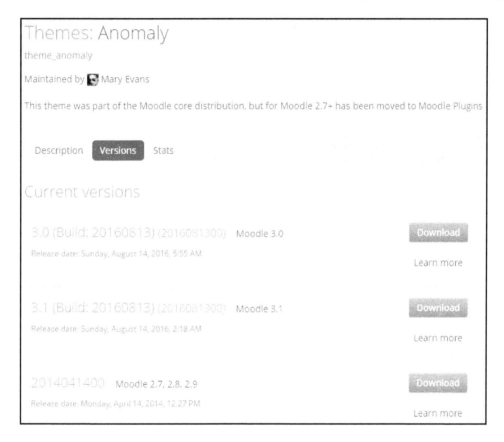

Shoelace

Shoelace is available for Moodle 3.1 and Moodle 3 as well as earlier Moodle versions. It allows color scheme adaptation and contains thin fonts, and can be downloaded from, `http s://moodle.org/plugins/pluginversions.php?plugin=theme_shoelace`:

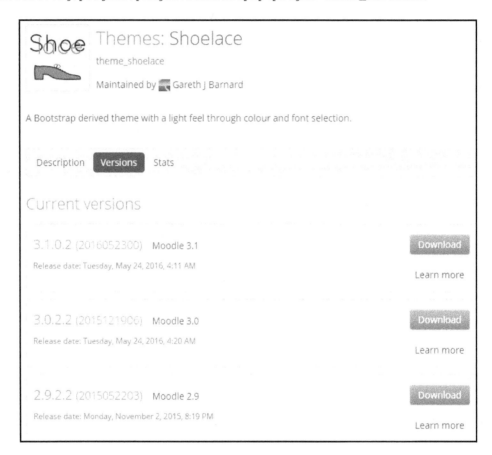

Flexpage

Flexpage is available for Moodle 3 as well as earlier Moodle versions. It has a new and improved layout of the course format, and can be downloaded from, `https://moodle.org /plugins/pluginversions.php?plugin=theme_flexpage`:

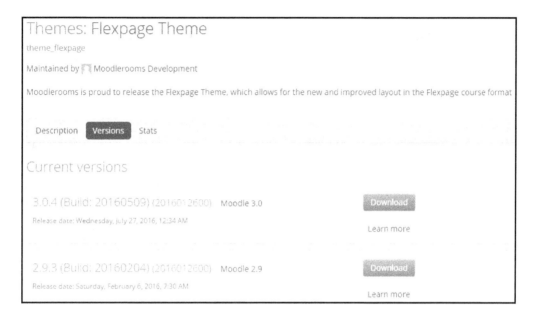

Overlay

Overlay is available for Moodle 3.1 and Moodle 3 as well as earlier Moodle versions. It has a three-column layout that displays the content to the left of both block columns; therefore, it is a non-traditional theme. It can be downloaded from, `https://moodle.org/plugins/pl` `uginversions.php?plugin=theme_overlay`:

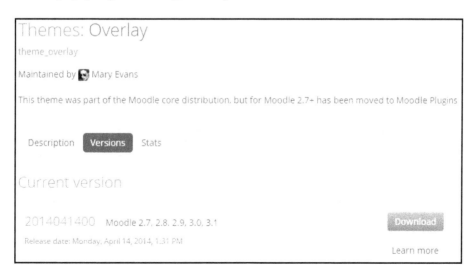

Comparing and contrasting all the themes

The following chart lists all the themes that we have been working with and that are available at the time of writing for Moodle 3.1 and Moodle 3. There are plenty that are also available for earlier versions. They are compared and contrasted so that we can choose the one that caters to our needs:

Theme	Academic use	Corporations, companies, and professionals	Personal use	Two columns	Website	Miscellaneous
Essential		Yes			Yes (homepage)	
Contemporary	Yes	Yes				
Aadvark	Yes (modern student)					
Academi	Yes (students)					
Adaptable	Yes (university)	Yes (training companies)		Yes		
Klass	Yes (e-learning)					
Eguru	Yes (educational establishments)					
Archaius						Several options to customize
Elegance				Yes		
Pioneer	Yes (learning content)					
Boostrap						CSS framework
Dynamic	Yes		Yes			
Roshnilite						Customizable sections
Campus						Customizable

Eduhub	Yes (educational purposes)				
Morecandy					Customizable, similar to More
Crisp				Yes	
Ulkit					Easily customized
Rocket		Yes			
Aigne					Perfect for slower Internet locations
Shoeborn		Yes			
Flexibase					Create layout
Snap	Yes (online learning)				
Decaf					Easy navigation
Afterburner					Moodle core distribution
Bootswatch					Child theme
Cerulean					Child theme
Splash					Moodle core distribution
Serenity					Moodle core distribution
Anomaly					Moodle core distribution
Shoelace					Light feel
Sharp	Yes	Yes	Yes	Yes	
Flexpage					Improved layout

Overlay						Moodle core distribution

Test your knowledge

A. These themes can be used for corporations, professionals, and companies …

    1. …essential, Contemporary, Adaptable, Sharp, Shoeborn, and Rocket.

    2. …essential, Contemporary, Adaptable, Snap, Shoelace, and Rocket.

    3. …essential, Contemporary, Anomaly, Snap, Shoelace, and Rocket.

B. A child theme is a theme that …

    1. …inherits the functions and styles from anther parent theme.

    2. …does not inherit the functions and styles from anther parent theme.

    3. …does not work with Moodle.

C. Cerulean and Bootswatch are …

    1. …parent themes.

    2. …child themes.

    3. …not available at the moment of the writing.

D. Both Dynamic and Sharp are themes that can be used for …

    1. …academic and personal use.

    2. …websites and personal use.

    3. …professional and personal use.

E. All of the themes in the chapter are …

    1. …available free of charge at `https://moodle.org/plugins/browse.php?list=category&id=3`.

    2. …paid and available at `https://moodle.org/plugins/browse.php?list=category&id=3`.

    3. …free of charge and are already installed when we download Moodle on-premises.

Summary

In this chapter, we have dealt with all the themes available for Moodle 3.1 and Moodle 3, which are free of charge and downloadable at `https://moodle.org/plugins/browse.php ?list=category&id=3`. We have changed the look and feel of our Moodle course several times in order to show how it looks dressed in other themes. We will go on exploring more theme details in the following chapter.

9
Course Formats

In the previous chapter, we have worked with the look and feel of our Moodle course in order to enhance it; now it is time to pay attention to course formats. Course formats are plugins that determine the layout of course resources. They are also important for proper sequencing and successful navigation so that instructional materials are connected to learning objectives. They determine how the course main page looks. The organization of the content of the course is also related to course formats.

There are some default course formats and a course format plugin, which allows different layouts and structures for course activities; we will explore all of them throughout the chapter. In this chapter, we will focus on **course formats**. By default, both Moodle on-premises and MoodleCloud come with four course formats:

- Weekly format
- Topics format
- Social format
- Single activity format

We will explain the differences and uses of these course formats. We will also work with the plugins available at the time of writing. We will explore the course formats that we can use in order to change and enhance our Moodle course.

The course format is used to display course items with different layouts and structures; as previously stated in this book, the course format that we are going to choose depends on the type of course that we are designing. Therefore, we will show how our Moodle course looks using some of the course formats, and we will compare and contrast them to understand when we can use each format.

We can choose a course format when we create a Moodle course; therefore, we will start from scratch to create a course and select the desired course format. In this case, we will select from among the default ones, and we will see how the course looks according to the type that we choose to use.

There are also several course format plugins. We will explore the course formats available for Moodle 3 and 3.1 at the time of writing. These plugins can be downloaded and installed in Moodle on-premises, but they do not work for MoodleCloud.

In this chapter, we shall:

- Create a Moodle course
- Explore the topic of course formats
- Change a course format
- Download a course format plugin
- Select the Grid course format
- Explore plugin course formats for Moodle 3 and 3.1

Creating a Moodle course

Before creating the Moodle course, we have to bear in mind the audience, so that we can decide on certain aspects of its appearance, such as the course format, which is the topic that we are dealing with throughout the book. Therefore, in this example, we will create a Moodle course for this chapter, **Course formats;** its audience is Moodlers who want to learn about theming. We will use Moodle on-premises and the steps are the same for MoodleCloud.

In order to design the new course, we have to enter Moodle and log in. Then, follow these steps:

1. Click on **Turn editing on**.
2. Click on **Add a new course**, as shown in the following screenshot:

3. Complete the necessary blocks to create the course.
4. Scroll down until you get to **Course format**.
5. Under **Course format**, **Format** appears. Click on the downward arrow next to **Format** and select **Single activity format**, as shown in the following screenshot:

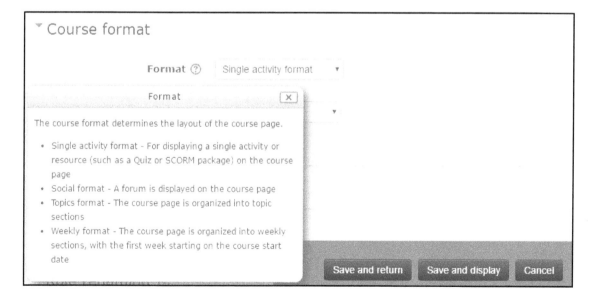

If you click on the question mark next to the format, a pop-up window appears displaying information about the default course formats available in both MoodleCloud and Moodle on-premises.

In this case, the **Single activity format** centers on one activity; when you click on **Single activity format**, a drop-down menu appears displaying the activity that you want to create. We must bear in mind that there must be no activities in the course when we choose this type of format.

After selecting, choose an activity to create in the Moodle course.

6. Scroll down the page and, within **Appearance**, **Force theme** appears.
7. Click on the downward arrow next to **Force theme** and click on **Essential**, which is the current theme on the sample Moodle course. It is shown in the following screenshot:

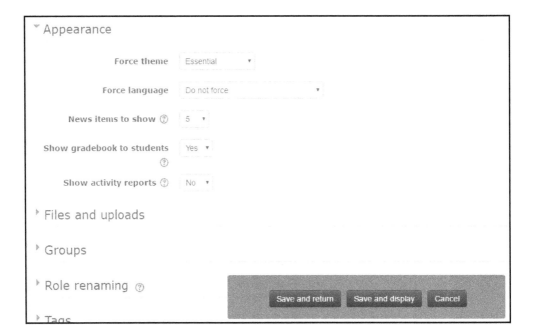

8. Enroll users for this course, if there aren't any.
9. The course looks as shown in the following screenshot:

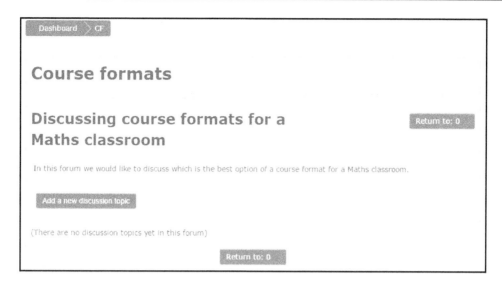

Exploring the topic course format

Within the courses in our Moodle on-premises, we have already designed two courses. The first course that we designed is Moodle 3 Theme Development. It was created using topics; therefore, we can group activities related to specific subjects. The available courses are shown in the following screenshot:

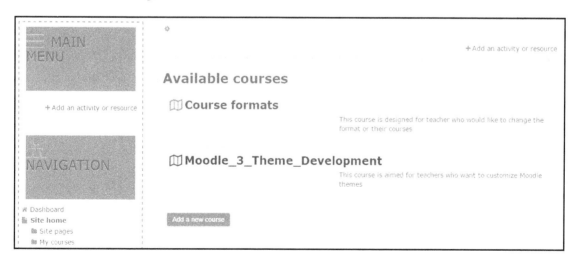

We will edit the topics section in the Moodle course. Before doing this, we need to be in editing mode, so click on **Turn editing on**. Afterwards, follow these steps in order to edit the topics within the **Moodle_3_Theme_Development** course:

1. Click on the **Moodle_3_Theme_Development** course, the course created, or the course on **Course formats**.
2. Choose topic to edit.
3. Click on the downward arrow next to **Edit** and click on **Edit topic**, as shown in the following screenshot:

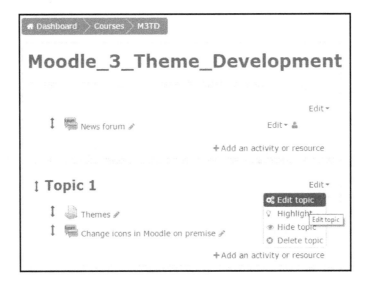

4. Click on the tick next to **Use default section name [Topic 1]**, so as to write the name of the topic; it is shown in the following screenshot:

5. Enter a name in the **Section name** field.

6. Complete the **Summary** block.
7. Click on **Save changes**.
8. Click on **Turn editing on**.
9. The course looks as shown in the following screenshot:

10. Repeat Steps 2 to 7 to change the names of the other topics.

Changing a course format

We have already dealt with two default course formats, Single Activity and topics. It is time to learn how to change a course format if we realize that it does not work the way we have designed it. Another option is that, as time goes by, we need to group activities or resources; therefore, it is a good excuse to change the course format. These are the steps that we have to follow:

1. Log in to the Moodle course.

2. Click on **Turn editing off**.

3. Under **Site administration**, click on **Courses | Manage courses and categories**, as shown in the following screenshot:

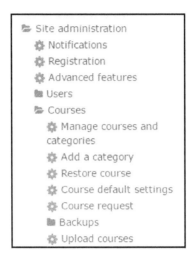

4. Click on a course to edit it, as shown in the following screenshot:

5. Click on **Course format**.

6. Click on the downward arrow next to **Format**.

7. Click on **Weekly format**, as shown in the following screenshot:

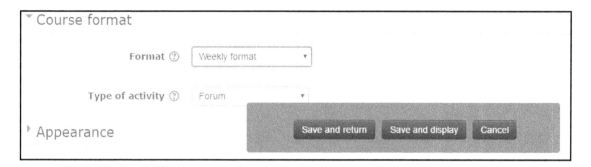

8. Click on **Save and display**.
9. Click on **Turn editing off**.
10. The course looks as shown in the following screenshot:

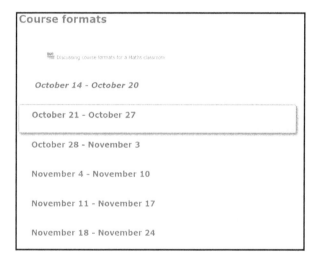

11. Repeat steps 2 to 6.
12. Click on **Social format**, as shown in the following screenshot:

13. Click on **Save and display**.
14. Click on **Turn editing off**.
15. The course looks as shown in the following screenshot:

Downloading a course format plugin

We have already explored the four default course formats within our Moodle course. Therefore, if we need to design a course with another type of course format, we can download it from the following website: `https://moodle.org/plugins/browse.php?list=category&id=19`. On this website, we can choose from several free and open source course formats.

We can only download course format plugins for Moodle on-premises; we can't work with plugins for MoodleCloud. It is the same with themes; they can be downloaded for Moodle on-premises, but they don't work on MoodleCloud. Thus, this section will deal only with Moodle on-premises.

Based on the Moodle version that we are using, a similar version course format plugin can be downloaded. It works in a similar way to themes. Therefore, in this section, we will download the **Grid course format**. Follow these steps in order to download it:

1. Enter the following website: `https://moodle.org/plugins/browse.php?list=category&id=19`.
2. Click on **Grid Format**.
3. Click on **Download**, as shown in the following screenshot:

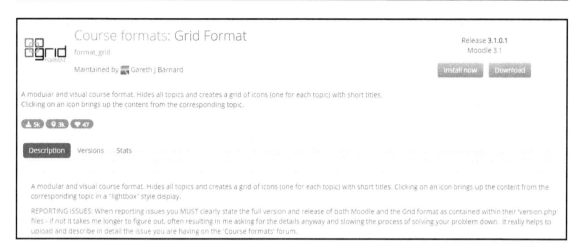

4. After downloading the file, copy and paste it into the
   `server\moodle\course\format` directory, as shown in the following
   screenshot:

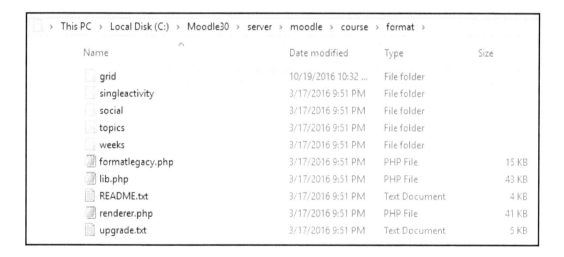

You will find the four default course format files within this directory: single activity, social, topics, and weeks (aka weekly).

5. Log in to Moodle on-premises and you will find what is shown in the following screenshot:

6. Click on **Upgrade Moodle database now**, as shown in the previous screenshot.
7. The installation was successful, so click on **Continue**, as shown in the following screenshot:

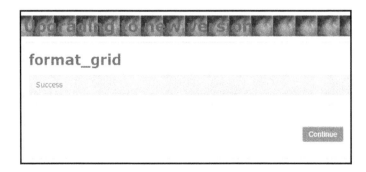

8. You can change or edit the setting of the grid course format. Afterwards, click on **Save changes**, as shown in the following screenshot:

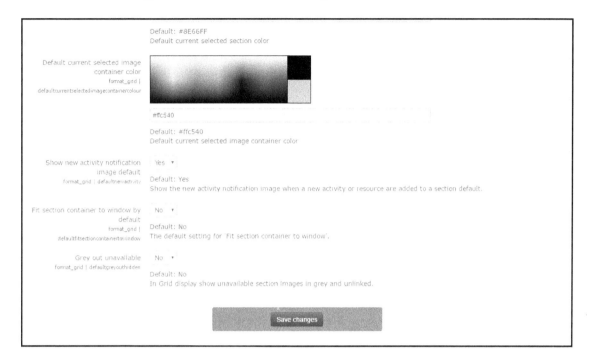

Selecting the Grid course format

We have just installed the Grid course format plugin in the previous section, so we will change course formats and select the course format that we have already downloaded. The **Grid course format** is a modular and visual course format. It creates a grid of icons with short titles. In order to change the course format, we have to complete the following steps:

1. Log on to the Moodle course.
2. Under **Site administration** click on **Courses | Manage courses and categories**.
3. Click on the desired course to change the format.
4. Click on **Course format**.
5. Click on the downward arrow next to **Format** and choose **Grid** as shown in the following screenshot:

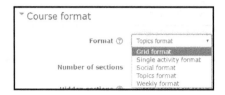

6. There are several items that you can edit within the Grid course format, so, after editing, click on **Save and display**.

7. The course looks as shown in the following screenshot:

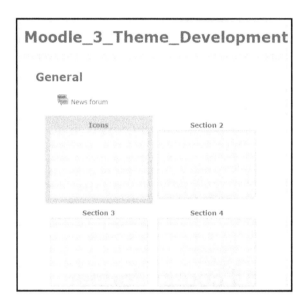

8. When you click on any of the grid icons, it brings up the contents from the corresponding topic. This is shown in the following screenshot:

9. When you click on the sideways arrows, you can change sections.

Exploring plugin course formats

There are several course formats that we can download from the following website: `https://moodle.org/plugins/browse.php?list=category&id=19`. They change the look and feel of the Moodle course, and the layout for displaying courses. In this section, we will explore the different course formats that we can download. We will focus on the formats that are available at the time of writing for Moodle 3 and Moodle 3.1.

Collapsed topics

This course format is useful when a course has several topics or weeks. It can be downloaded from the following website: `https://moodle.org/plugins/format_topcoll`. In the event where we want to use this course format, we click on **Download** and follow the steps mentioned in the previous section.

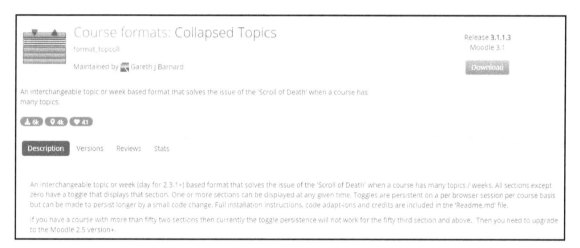

Socialwall format

This course format will turn the Moodle course into a social learning platform. There are many items that can be edited. We can download this course format from the following website: `https://moodle.org/plugins/format_socialwall`. With this format, we can create posts and write comments similarly to how this is done on social networks.

If we want to download the **Socialwall** course format, we click on **Download**, as shown in the following screenshot:

Onetopic format

In this type of format, each topic is shown in a tab. We can download it from the following website: `https://moodle.org/plugins/format_onetopic`. If we want to download the Onetopic format, we click on **Download**, as shown in the following screenshot:

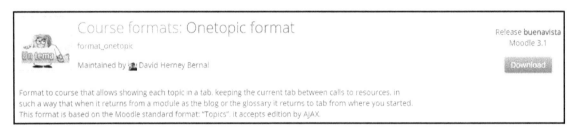

MindMap format

In this type of course format, we convert the Moodle course into a MindMap. It is quite appealing for different purposes. In the event where we want to download the **MindMap Format** course, we can do it from the following website: `https://moodle.org/plugins/fo rmat_mindmap`, as shown in the following screenshot:

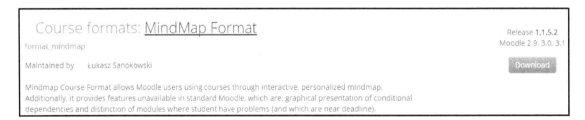

Periods format

This type of course format makes each section set a duration for a certain period of time in days, weeks, or months. We can download the **Periods format** from the following website: `https://moodle.org/plugins/format_periods`. If we want to use this course format, we click on **Download**, as shown in the following screenshot:

Course formats: Periods format

format_periods

Maintained by Marina Glancy

This course format allows to set duration for each section (period) in days, weeks, months or years. Each individual section (period) may override this duration. The course settings allow automatically collapse or hide past or future periods.

Release **3.0.3**
Moodle 3.0, 3.1

Download

Flexible sections format

This type of course format organizes the content of the course in a nested way. The sections can be expanded or collapsed. We can download the **Flexible section format** from the following website: `https://moodle.org/plugins/format_flexsections`. If we want to use this format, we click on **Download**, as shown in the following screenshot:

Course formats: Flexible sections format

format_flexsections

Maintained by Marina Glancy

Organises course content in any number of sections that can be nested. Each section can be displayed expanded or collapsed

Release **2.8.4**
Moodle 2.8, 2.9, 3.0, 3.1

Download

Buttons format

This course format has the menu designed with buttons. We can find this course format on the following website: `https://moodle.org/plugins/format_buttons`. If we want to download this course format, we click on **Download**, as shown in the following screenshot:

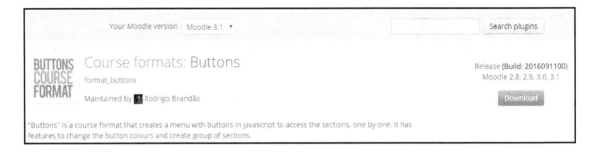

Board (Grid and Blocks) format

This type of course format has flexibility between sections and columns. We can download this course format from the following website: `https://moodle.org/plugins/format_boa rd`. If we want to download this course format, we click on **Download**, as shown in the following screenshot:

Mansonry topics format

This type of course format displays sections with a brick wall at the back. Each section can have a different background. We can download this course format from the following website: `https://moodle.org/plugins/format_masonry`. If we want to download this course format, we click on **Download**, as shown in the following screenshot:

eTask topics format

This type of course format is based on topics and has a grading table on the top of the course. It can be downloaded from the following website: `https://moodle.org/plugins/format_etask`. If we want to download this course format, we click on **Download**, as shown in the following screenshot:

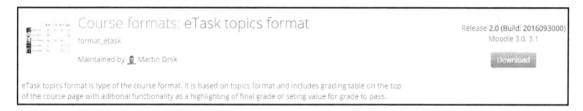

Menutopic format

In this type of course format, we can display topics or sections as a menu. We can download it from the following website: `https://moodle.org/plugins/format_menutopic`. To download this course format, we click on **Download**, as shown in the following screenshot:

Flexpage format

In this type of course format, the teacher can create a set of pages or subpages. We can download this course format from the following website: `https://moodle.org/plugins/pluginversions.php?plugin=format_flexpage`.

To download this course format, we click on **Download**, as shown in the following screenshot:

GPS format

This type of course format allows content to be displayed according to the geographical coordinates of the learner. It is available for Moodle 3 and earlier versions. It can be downloaded from the following website: `https://moodle.org/plugins/pluginversions.php?plugin=format_gps`. To download this course format, we click on **Download**, as shown in the following screenshot:

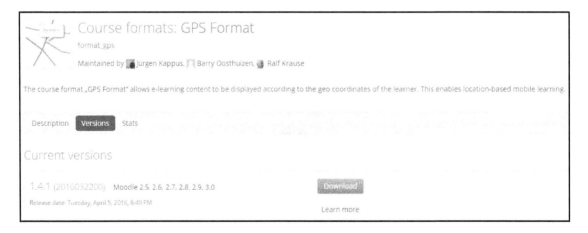

Columns format

In this type of format, we can choose the number of columns to use in the Moodle course. It gives a journalistic feel, though. It is available for Moodle 3 as well as for earlier versions. It can be downloaded from the following website: `https://moodle.org/plugins/pluginversions.php?plugin=format_columns`. To download this course format, we click on **Download**, as shown in the following screenshot:

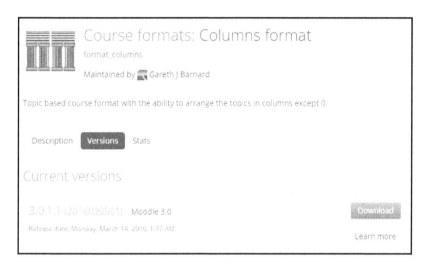

Noticeboard format

This type of course format displays the latest forum-post news at the top. It is available for Moodle 3 and earlier versions. It can be downloaded from the following website: `https://moodle.org/plugins/pluginversions.php?plugin=format_noticebd`.

To download this course format, we click on **Download**, as shown in the following screenshot:

Folder view format

This type of format displays both activities and resources within a folder, which can be expanded or collapsed. It is available for Moodle 3 and earlier versions. It can be downloaded from the following website: `https://moodle.org/plugins/pluginversions.php?plugin=format_folderview`. To download this course format, we click on **Download**, as shown in the following screenshot:

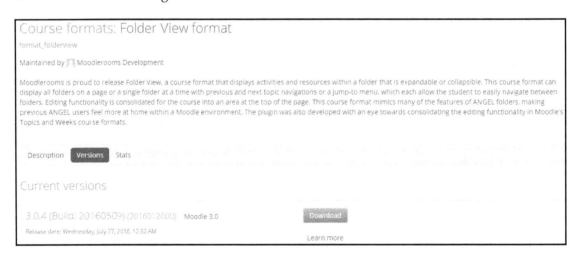

NED tabs course format

This type of course format displays either sections or weeks as numbered tabs. The tabs are unlimited and they can have different colors because they can be customized. It is available for Moodle 3 and 3.1 as well as for earlier versions. It can be downloaded from the following website: `https://moodle.org/plugins/pluginversions.php?plugin=format_f ntabs`. To download this course format, we click on **Download**, as shown in the following screenshot:

Test your knowledge

A. The course format determines …

1. …the layout of the course page.
2. …the theme.
3. …the activities of the page.

B. The default course formats are …

    1. …grid and Social format.

    2. …single activity, Social, Topics and weekly format.

    3. …social and Topic format.

C. When we select the Topic course format …

    1. …we can name the section or list the topics by default.

    2. …we number the sections, but we can't edit the names of the sections.

    3. …we can't edit the topics at all.

D. Once we select a course format …

    1. …we can't change it.

    2. …we can edit it and change it.

    3. …we need to install a plugin to change it.

E. Course formats can be downloaded and …

    1. …uploaded to Moodle on-premises so that they can be chosen.

    2. …they work in both Moodle on-premises and MoodleCloud.

    3. …they work.

Summary

In summary, in this chapter we have dealt with course formats. There are default course formats and there are also plugins for them. These course formats can be downloaded from the Moodle website and they can be installed in Moodle on-premises. We can also change the format of our courses in order to enhance it and make the course a little bit different. We have to bear in mind what type of course we need to create in order to choose the right course format. In the final chapter, we will put all the pieces together.

10
Extending Moodle Theming to Specific Sections

In this chapter, we will put together many pieces of the theming puzzle. We will take advantage of all the features that we have already dealt with and we will enhance them a little bit more by adding special elements or ingredients. Once the theme is set, we can develop its content taking into account all the elements that we have changed throughout the book. Said elements are tips which help us to organize course content, and adding blocks to enhance a theme, among others. Overall, this chapter will help you to create a more effective Moodle course.

We will extend Moodle theming by giving some tips, once we have made the necessary changes to the theme in the Moodle course. These changes are important to bear in mind when designing a Moodle course or while theming a Moodle course. Therefore, we will go over each of the chapters and we will add another element or ingredient to our Moodle course. That is to say, we will combine what we have covered previously and we will continue changing its look and feel.

In this chapter, we shall:

- Put all the pieces together
- Organize course content
- Add blocks to enhance a theme
- Upload a logo in a description section
- Social networks, header, footer, and breadcrumb style
- Coding with CSS in Moodle
- Logos, images, and icons
- Dealing with different devices
- Course formats and layouts
- The result

Putting all the pieces together

Here is a recap of what we have already covered in the previous chapters

In Chapter 1, *An Introduction to Moodle 3 and MoodleCloud*, we covered most of what needs to be known about e-learning, VLEs and Moodle, and MoodleCloud. There is a slight difference between Moodle and MoodleCloud especially if you don't have access to a Moodle course in the institution where you are working and want to design a Moodle course. Furthermore, Moodle is used in different devices and there are several aspects to take into account when designing a course and building a Moodle theme. We have also dealt with screen resolution, aspect ratio, types of images and text, and anti-aliasing effects.

In Chapter 2, *Themes in Moodle 3 and MoodleCloud*, we learned about what themes are and how to find them in Moodle and in MoodleCloud. We also explored a little about HTML code and how colors are named in this code. We also customized the "More" Moodle theme and found out where our Moodle themes are in our computer. We searched for, downloaded, and installed the "Essential" Moodle theme. We dealt with plenty of information relevant to Moodle themes and where to find it.

In Chapter 3, *Setting Up Logos in Moodle Themes*, we worked with UI-based settings to tune our Moodle themes. We did not have to make changes to specific files such as HTML files or CSS because we used a theme where we could upload a logo, favicon, and background image as a tiled style. We have made all these changes in Moodle on-premises.

With regard to MoodleCloud, we uploaded a logo, which could be seen in the headers of the front page and login page, allowed by the theme that we are working with, bearing in mind that MoodleCloud has some limitations.

In `Chapter 4`, *Customizing the Header and the Footer*, we learnt how to add images and text to the footer and the header. Hence, we also added hyperlinks to social networks in Moodle on-premises. Apart from that, we added slide shows and modified the front page, changing the look and feel of the Moodle course. We made some changes to MoodleCloud, taking into account its limitations using customizable areas.

In `Chapter 5`, *Customizing Elements with CSS*, we worked with several online text editors to learn more about CSS and what we can do in order to change the look and feel of Moodle on-premises. We also tested the code before making any changes and avoiding making mistakes. The look and feel of Moodle is completely different from the one that we had at the beginning of this book, so we kept on making changes.

In `Chapter 6`, *Locating, Editing and Using New Icons*, we worked with icons. We also worked with vector graphics and bitmaps. We modified SVG files and exported them as PNG files. We changed the look and feel of the Moodle on-premises course and we personalized the icon. We can also add more images to the icons or edit them in a different way, but we always have to follow the steps that we have taken. We need to make copies of files and replace the edited files with the originals. We may not like how the new icon looks in the Moodle course. We kept on personalizing our Moodle on-premises course.

In `Chapter 7`, *Optimizing Themes for Mobile Devices*, we worked with emulators for mobile devices, we also checked Internet connectivity and we learned how to modify, edit, and customize some of these options. We worked with Google DevTools, which is an online emulator, and learnt how to work with a mobile device from either our desktop or laptop. Moreover, we emulated network connectivity to check how the theme downloads on a mobile device.

We can customize, not only the device, but also its connectivity. When throttling the connectivity we can see the speed. In the next chapter, we will continued theming our Moodle course.

In `Chapter 8`, *Exploring Layouts*, we dealt with all the themes available for Moodle 3.1 and Moodle 3, which are free of charge and downloadable at `https://moodle.org/plugins/browse.php?list=category&id=3`. We changed the look and feel of our Moodle course several times in order to show how it looks dressed in other themes.

In `Chapter 9`, *Course formats*, we dealt with course formats. There are default course formats and there is also a plugin for them. These course formats can be downloaded from the Moodle website and they can be installed in Moodle on-premises. We can also change the course format of our courses in order to enhance them and make the courses a little bit different. We have to bear in mind what type of course we need to create in order to choose the right course format.

Organizing course content

When we create or design a course from scratch, we have to bear in mind how to organize content, as well as consider the methodology that we will apply for teaching the students. Therefore, we organize the resources and the activities approximately.

We can arrange all the resources together or we can switch between resources and activities. We should provide students with content before designing an activity. Therefore, by taking advantage of Moodle's abundance of different resources and activities, we can create a variety of content for our Moodle course.

To organize the course content, we will work on the *Course formats* course, which was created in the previous chapter. Follow these steps to organize the course content:

1. Enter the Moodle course and log in.
2. Click on **Turn editing on**.
3. Click on **Edit** | **Edit topic** within a topic block, as shown in the following screenshot:

4. Complete the **Section name** block, untick the block next to **Use default section name [Topic 1]**.
5. Complete the **Summary** block.

6. Click on **Save changes**, as shown in the following screenshot:

7. Click on **Add an activity or resource | File | Add**.
8. Complete the **Name** block.
9. Complete the **Description** block, tick the block **Display description on course page**.
10. Under **Content**, upload the files concerning the topic.
11. Click on **Appearance**.
12. Click on **Show more...**.
13. There are some aspects to consider for displaying the file. They are shown in the following screenshot:

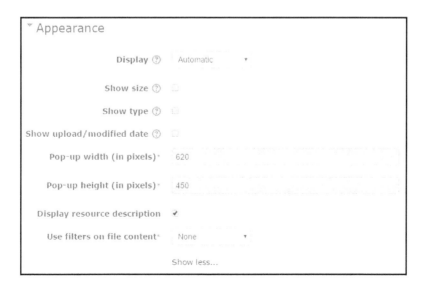

14. Click on **Save and return to course**, as shown in the following screenshot:

15. Click on **Add an activity or resource** I **URL** I **Add**.
16. Complete the **Name** and **Description** blocks.
17. Tick the block that reads **Display description on course page**.
18. Click on **Content** and write the **URL** for the resource.
19. Click on **Appearance** and verify that the chosen options are the ones desired.

20. Click on **Save and return to course**, as shown in the following screenshot:

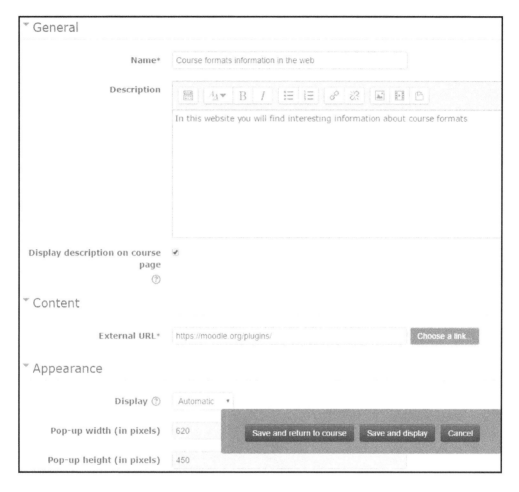

21. Click on **Add an activity or resource** | **Glossary** | **Add**.
22. Complete the **Name** and **Description** blocks.
23. Tick the block that reads **Display description on course page**.
24. Click on **Entries.** Customize it.
25. Click on **Appearance**. Customize its appearance.

26. Click on **Save and return to course**, as shown in the following screenshot:

We have written a name for the topic of the course. After that, we have added two resources and then an activity, that is to say, that the course content is organized. Therefore, the course looks as shown in the following screenshot:

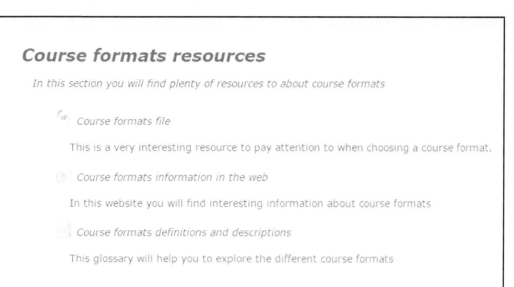

Adding blocks to enhance a theme

Once the content is organized, we may customize the theme or change the theme that we are using. We have already dealt with themes in Chapter 2, *Themes in Moodle 3 and MoodleCloud*, therefore in this section we will not be changing the theme, but we will be adding elements to it. The elements that we will add are blocks. Blocks are where the instructional material is incorporated.

One of the reasons for choosing a specific theme for a course is the target audience. In the previous example, the audience are Moodlers who would like to learn about course formats, so we can add some blocks to the theme in order to enhance the look and feel of the Moodle course.

There are several types of blocks, which can be added to the Moodle course. We can enhance the course in a simple way by adding useful elements within blocks for the user of the course. We enter our Moodle course and log in, and afterwards when we click on **Turn editing on**, an option appears to add a block. There are different types of blocks to add. They are listed and briefly explained in the following table:

Type of block	Characteristics
Activities	Lists and allows navigation between the different activities available in the course. When there is a different activity or resource to the course, an icon will appear.
Activity result	It displays results from the activities that are graded or rated in a course.
Admin bookmark	It bookmarks pages, and the administrator role can see them as a list of links.
Blog menu	It provides links to view all entries or add a new entry.
Blog tags	It displays a list of blogs where the font size visually indicates the use of the blog. The blog that is more frequently used appears in a larger font size.
Calendar	It displays the site event, the course event, group events, and the user personal event.
Comments	It can be added to any page to allow users to add comments.
Community finder	It enables users to access public community hubs and search for courses to download or enroll on.
Course completion status	It shows what has been done to complete the course.
Course overview	It is on a user's home page and it shows a list of the courses on which the user is enrolled.
Course site summary	It provides a summary or description for the course set in the summary text of the course settings.
Courses	Lists and allows navigation between all the courses in which the logged in user is a participant.
Feedback	It provides a quick link to global feedback activities set up from the front page.
Flickr	It allows users to change the images displayed in the block based on relevance, date, interest, and date taken.

Global search	It allows users to search the site for specific content. This is a new feature in Moodle 3.1.
HTML	It is a block used to add text or images. It is the most customizable block and it can incorporate a variety of functions and uses. It has a standard text editor thus; we can also work with HTML code as well.
Latest announcements	It displays the recent posts made in the announcement forum, as well as the link to older archived news.
Latest badges	It displays the badges earned on the course.
Learning plans	It gives users quick access to different learning plans that they may have.
Logged in user	It displays certain information about the user who is currently logged in to a Moodle course.
Login	It provides logged out users an in-site area to enter the username, password, and login. They can also create a new account or reset their password.
Main menu	It can be added to the front page of the site, therefore resources and activities can be added to the front page.
Mentees (parents who have access to the children's information through the link in the block)	It is a front page block that provides mentors with a quick access to their mentee profile page.
Messages	It displays a list of new messages received with a link to a messages window.
My private files	It enables access to a user's private files area.
Navigation	It contains a menu that includes My Home, Site pages, My profile, and Courses.
Network servers	It allows users to roam to other Moodle servers.
Online users	It shows a list of users who have been logged into the current course. The list is updated every five minutes.
People	It contains a link to the list of participants associated with the Moodle course area in various roles.

Quiz result	It displays the highest and or lowest grades achieved on a quiz within a course. It is essential that there is a quiz in the course to configure this block.
Random glossary entry	It can be used to display random entries from a glossary, which has the form of dictionary style definitions.
Recent activity	It shows activity since a user last access to the course, and a full report of recent activity.
Recent blog entries	It can be configured to display the last N blog entries, which can be filtered by context.
Remote RSS feeds	It enables RSS feeds from external websites to be displayed within the Moodle course.
Search forums	It allows you to search the course forums for a word or phrase.
Section links	It helps the student or teacher to quickly navigate to a particular topic/week section of the course.
Self completion	It provides a link for students to manually declare that they have completed the course.
Social activities	It enables additional activities to be added to a course in a social format.
Tags	It is a feature of tag clouds, which depending on the size of each tag, is related to the number of items associated with it. The larger the tag, the more items associated with it.
Upcoming events	It displays future events in a summarized list.
YouTube	It will pull YouTube videos with the same tag words as the tags page it is on.

In some cases, the previously listed blocks belong to a plugin, which needs an API key to work. Most of the blocks can be added when turning editing on, whereas others such as YouTube, need an API. For more information on how blocks work on Moodle, we can visit: `https://docs.moodle.org/31/en/Blocks`.

In this example, we will add a calendar block to change the look and feel of our course. To do so, follow these steps:

1. Enter the Moodle course and log in.
2. Click on **Turn editing on**.
3. Click on **ADD A BLOCK** | **Calendar**, as shown in the following screenshot:

4. Click on **Action** | **Configure calendar block**.
5. Configure the calendar block (in which pages the block appears and where).

6. Click on **Save changes**, as shown in the following screenshot:

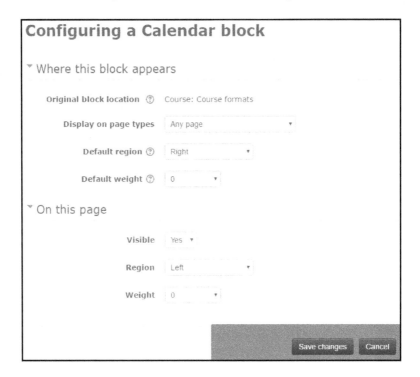

7. Another option is to click on the Move calendar block icon and place the block in another part of the page, as shown in the following screenshot:

There are a great variety of blocks, which can enhance the look and feel of the Moodle course. It would take a whole chapter to talk about all of them, and thus we will not cover them all. The idea is that we have to bear in mind that some blocks can help to create an attractive course. Furthermore, in some cases, resources or activities can be designed in blocks.

8. Click on **Turn editing off** and the course should look as shown in the following screenshot:

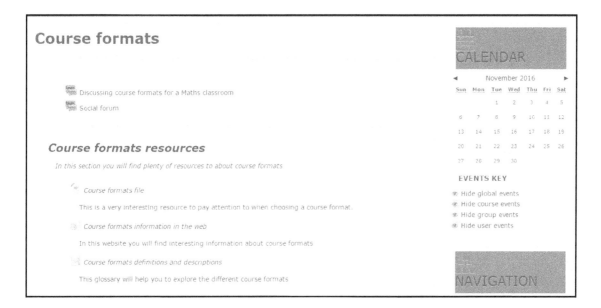

Uploading a logo in a description section

In Chapter 3, *Setting Up Logos in Moodle Themes*, we dealt with logos in Moodle. Therefore, as an example, our Moodle course has its own logo. So, we will use the same logo and add it to the description of a section. It is very attractive to start the section of a course with a logo that previews the topics that the students are going to deal with. We can also add a combination of images to create a new image, to define the section of a course.

To add a logo to our section, follow these steps:

1. Enter the Moodle course and log in.
2. Click on **Turn editing off**.
3. Click on **Edit** | **Edit section**, as shown in the following screenshot:

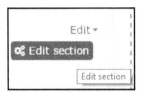

4. Complete the **Section Name**, and untick the block that reads **Use default section name [General]**.
5. In the **Summary** block, click on insert an image, and upload the logo or the desired image to be inserted in the section.
6. Complete the necessary blocks and click on **Save image**, as shown in the following screenshot:

7. The logo appears in the Summary block.

8. Click on **Save changes**, as shown in the following screenshot:

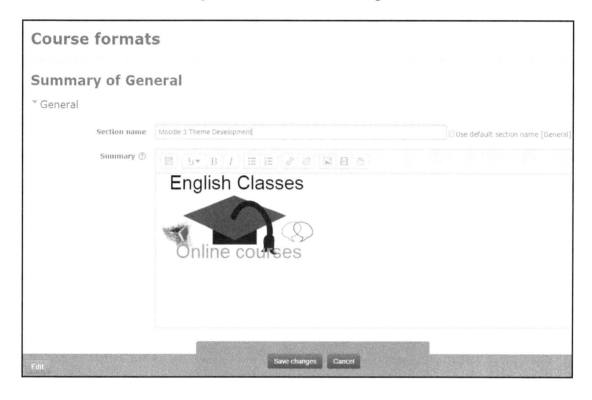

9. Click on **Turn editing off**. The Moodle course should look as shown in the following screenshot:

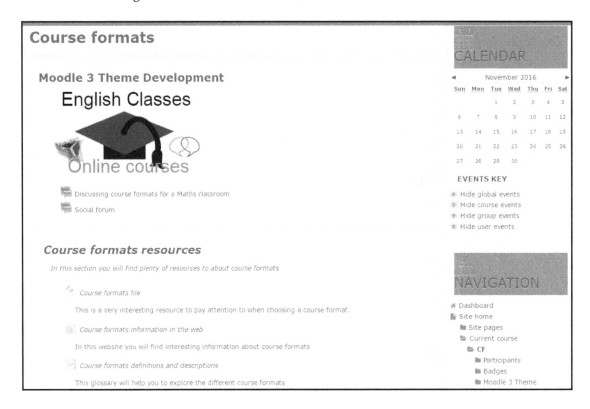

Social networks, headers, footers, and breadcrumb styles

In Chapter 4, *Customizing the Header and the Footer,* we changed the look and feel of the Moodle course by adding some elements to the header and the footer. Since the Moodle course always represents a place such as an institution or a company, we may include some elements that belong to it. Therefore, we have already covered in Chapter 4, *Customizing the Header and the Footer,* how to customize the header and the footer. We dealt with both MoodleCloud and Moodle on-premises.

We added a footnote in MoodleCloud. We also embedded social networks buttons to the header in Moodle on-premises using the Essential theme. We have customized the footer in Moodle on-premises using the Essential theme and we have edited the front-page area contents. Furthermore, we have created a slide show in the front-page area content. We can keep on customizing it and tailoring it according to where the Moodle course belongs.

In this section, we will change the breadcrumb style, to give a specific look or improve navigation within Moodle. When theming, we can choose from either style or functionality. The type of breadcrumb we choose depends on our audience. In order to do this, we have to enter Moodle on-premises and log in. Afterwards, follow these steps:

1. Under **Site administration**, click on **Appearance** | **Themes** | **Essential** | **Header**, as shown in the following screenshot:

2. Scroll down and four options will appear for the breadcrumb. Click on the breadcrumb style of your choice.
3. Click on **Save changes**, as shown in the following screenshot:

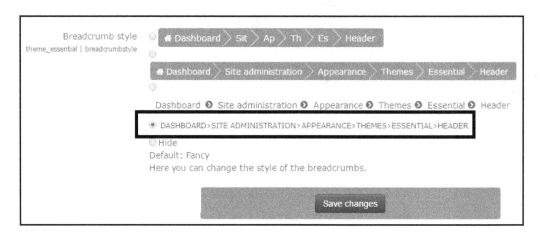

4. The Moodle on-premises course should look as shown in the following screenshot:

Coding with CSS in Moodle

In Chapter 5, *Customizing Elements with CSS*, we dealt with CSS code and we worked with some online editors which helped us with the coding. We can do plenty of things with coding and it would take an entire book or another chapter to edit CSS code. What we must bear in mind is that there is a block that allows us to use CSS code in order to edit what we need or desire. In most cases, HTML code is appropriate since it is also possible to edit HTML code when we add an activity or resource.

We have already dealt with CSS code in Chapter 5, *Customizing Elements with CSS*, and we can explore the resources in said chapter to improve and change the look and feel of the Moodle course. We have to bear in mind that we need a CSS block that allows us to edit such code, as was previously explained in said chapter.

Logos, images, and icons

Logos, images, and icons are essential elements to bear in mind and include in our Moodle course when changing the look and feel. We have been working with them throughout this chapter and we can also add more of them. Furthermore, when exploring several course formats, we came across the instances where images could be of great help. We always have the possibility to add an image in any HTML editor, whether we add an activity or resource, we make links to the images. Thus, explore the previous chapter to include logos, images, or change the Moodle icons to change the appearance of the course.

Dealing with different devices

In Chapter 7, *Optimizing Themes for Mobile Devices*, we emulated different devices in order to check how the theme looks/works on a mobile device. It is essential to check it, because there are many devices available and we need to test if what we have done works properly on both desktops and mobile devices. Therefore, any changes that we make to the look and feel of the Moodle course, we need to test by emulating them.

Course formats and layouts

We can download both free course formats and layouts from the following website: `https://moodle.org/plugins/browse.php?list=category&id=19`. We can combine both themes, and enhance and tailor our Moodle course according to our needs. It would be impossible to set a combination of both because we would need to explore a matching. In other words, we need to analyze what we need from our Moodle course and explore the formats and layouts to choose the best combination. In `Chapter 8`, *Exploring Layouts* and `Chapter 9`, *Course formats*, we have explored both of them, so choose one in combination with the other to theme our Moodle course.

The result

The result is what we want our Moodle course to be: in other words, it's important to review the results to assure navigation and user experience among other facts to take into account in order to achieve learning goals and institutional objectives. We need to focus on the audience and the company or school for whom the course is meant for, and afterwards there are plenty of items that can be customized in order to get the appropriate course. Throughout this book, we have explored many items and some ideas that can be used to enhance the look and the feel of the course.

Summary

In summary, in this chapter, we have combined all the elements that we have learnt throughout the chapters. We have also added some ingredients in some cases, which allows us to change the appearance of the Moodle course in order to customize it in the desired way.

Furthermore, we have explored different ways in which we can simply change the look and feel of the course, since we can just add blocks, images, or make some small changes to the Moodle course, which will allow us to see it in a different way.

Whenever we design an activity or add a resource, we must also bear in mind that we need to think of how to organize them, because the course will look tidier depending on how we organize the content. Therefore, enjoy theming your Moodle course while you teach or design your courses!

Test Your Knowledge Answers

This appendix contains answers to all the Test Your Knowledge quizzes that appear in the chapters. Now, let's have a look at the answers to the respective questions.

Chapter 1, An Introduction to Moodle 3 and MoodleCloud

Questions	Answers
A. Moodle is a learning platform through which …	**1.** …we can design, build and create E-learning environments.
B. BigBlueButtonBN …	**2.** …lets you create from within Moodle links to real-time online classrooms.
C. Moodle Cloud …	**2.** …does not allow more than 50 users.
D. The number of pixels the display of the device has horizontally and vertically and the color depth measuring the number of bits representing the color of each pixel make up…	**1.** …screen resolution.
E. Anti-aliasing can be applied to …	**3.** …both images and text.

Chapter 2, Themes in Moodle 3 on-premises and MoodleCloud

Questions	Answers
A. MoodleCloud offers …	**1.** …a restrictive number of themes because there are no plugins available.
B. More theme can be customized…	**2.** …directly from our Moodle on-premises course or MoodleCloud course using HTML tags.
C. Course themes …	**2.** …overrides user themes.
D. The Essential Moodle theme can be …	**1.** …downloaded from `www.moodle.org` and customized.
E. Mobiles app can be detected only if …	**3.** …the **Enable device detection** icon is ticked within **Theme settings**.

Chapter 3 Setting up Logos in Moodle Themes

Questions	Answers
A. We can see the logo in MoodleCloud theme More …	**1.** …in the header of the front page and on the login page.
B. If we add a logo to the Essential theme …	**2.** …we can see the logo in the header of all pages in the course.
C. Favicon is short for …	**1.** …favorite icon.
D. When we add a favicon …	**2.** …we have to download a `.ico` file.
E. Header background images can be set as tiled style …	**1.** …to cover all the header below the logo.

Chapter 4, Customizing the Header and the Footer

Questions	Answers
A. If we customize the footnote in MoodleCloud…	**1.** …we can see it throughout the course.
B. We can add links to social networks in Essential themes in Moodle on premise …	**2.** …adding the URL to the belonging blocks under Header within **Theme | Appearance**.
C. If we want to add an image to the footer …	**1.** …we can do it using HTML code.
D. When we customize the front page area we can see it on …	**2.** …site home.
E. We can add …	**1.** ..no more than 16 slides.

Chapter 5, Customizing Elements with CSS

Questions	Answers
A. To customize the size of an image …	**1.** …we need to edit CSS code.
B. The Essential theme lets us customize CSS …	**2.** …within the Site administration menu.
C. Course themes …	**2.** …can be partially customized.
D. The Essential Moodle theme …	**1.** …allows us to edit CSS.
E. Online editors …	**3.** …let us edit code and see the changes in order not to make mistakes in Moodle.

Chapter 6, Locating, Editing, and Using New Icons

Questions	Answers
A. We need to modify which file in order to see the changes in Moodle on-premises …	**1.** …the `.svg` file
B. We have to work with Inkscape …	**2.** …to edit an SVG file.
C. We need to check the number of pixels of which file that we have edited so that they match the same number of pixels of the original file/files …	**2.** …a PNG file
D. We have to rename …	**3.** …both the edited SVG file and the edited PNG file as the original.
E. It is advisable to keep a copy of …	**3.** …both the original PNG and SVG files.

Chapter 7, Optimizing Themes for Mobile Devices

Questions	Answers
A. We can enable Device Mode in Google Chrome by …	**1.** …pressing the *F12* key and clicking on the Toggle Device Toolbar icon.
B. We can edit an emulated device by selecting …	**2.** …devices.
C. In order to add a custom device, we need to complete …	**2.** …the device's name, width, and height blocks without exception.
D. When we throttle a network connectivity for the device …	**1.** …we simulate the Internet speed of the mobile device.
E. When we emulate network connectivity, we can …	**1.** …choose what we need to emulate.

Chapter 8, Exploring Layouts

Questions	Answers
A. These themes can be used for corporations, professionals, and companies…	**1.** …essential, Contemporary, Adaptable, Sharp, Shoeborn, and Rocket.
B. A child theme is a theme that …	**1.** …inherits the functions and styles from anther parent theme.
C. Cerulean and Bootswatch are …	**2.** …child themes.
D. Both Dynamic and Sharp are themes that can be used for …	**1.** …academic and personal use.
E. All of the themes in the chapter are …	**1.** …available free of charge at `https://moodle.org/plugins/browse.php?list=category&id=3`.

Chapter 9, Course Formats

Questions	Answers
A. The course format determines …	**1.** …the layout of the course page.
B. The default course formats are …	**2.** …single activity, Social, Topics, and weekly format.
C. When we select the Topic course format…	**1.** …we can name the section or list the topics by default.
D. Once we select a course format …	**2.** …we can edit it and change it.
E. Course formats can be downloaded and…	**1.** …uploaded to Moodle on-premises so that they can be chosen.

Index

www.ingramcontent.com/pod-product-compliance
Lightning Source LLC
Chambersburg PA
CBHW062112050326
40690CB00016B/3291